REVELATION
THE BIRTH OF A NEW AGE

by David

INTRODUCTION BY WILLIAM IRWIN THOMPSON

LORIAN PRESS

ISBN 0-936878-00-2

Published by The Lorian Press
A division of The Lorian Association
P.O. Box 1095
Elgin, Illinois 60120

Second Lorian Press Printing 1980.
Printed in the United States of America

DEDICATION

to

MYRTLE

and

To the Network of World Servers, Those Persons Who in their lives seek to be the co-creators of a new world, the living revelation of Limitless Love and Truth.

CONTENTS

PART IV: Revelation 1975

INTRODUCTION
by William Irwin Thompson

A generation ago Teilhard de Chardin made a prediction that has now become a cultural reality: "Like the meridians as they approach the poles, science, philosophy and religion are bound to converge as they draw nearer to the whole." [1.] It was a fanciful thought that Père Teilhard had in those dark postwar days in Paris when *le neant* seemed to be the ultimate expression of Western civilization, but now it is exciting to hear the scientist and the mystic speak in similar terms. In his new book, *The Survival of the Wisest*, Dr. Jonas Salk puts forth a theory of individual and group evolution that is remarkably similar to the work of David Spangler.

> My aim here is to suggest that the tendency toward the separation and isolation of human groups according to EGO values that have formed and prevailed until now has prevented the recognition and expression of the BEING. They have favored the association of individuals according to EGO values rather than BEING values. If, as is suspected from what has been happening in the human realm, BEING standards are emerging with EGO values appropriate thereto, removing the encumbrance of essentially foreign EGO values which contributed to the development of enormous internal and external conflicts, then Man is entering upon a new phase of his evolutionary development. [2.]

There are some playful ironies present in Dr. Salk's work, for, in many ways, he is dimly intuiting and vaguely expressing in his charts and graphs what is more clearly and substantially presented in Spangler's revelations. In a religious revelation, the concepts of evolution are expressed in emotional and spiritual imagery that enables all men to participate in a common mythology, but in a scientific expression of evolution, there is always a pronounced elitist tone that gives one pause. David Spangler has addressed himself directly to this problem, and his transmissions are very clear on the point that we go astray if we begin to think of mankind in terms of the apocalyptically damned and the millenial elect. Nevertheless, Dr. Salk's description of the new evolutionary vanguard seems to fit Findhorn more than the American Academy of Arts and Sciences:

A new body of conscious individuals exists, expressing its desire for a better life for Man as a species and as individuals, eager to devote themselves to this end. Such groups, when they are able to coalesce through an understanding of their relatedness to one another and to the natural processes involved in "Nature's game" of survival and evolution, will find strength and courage in sensing themselves as part of the Cosmos and as being involved in a game that is in accord with Nature and not anti-natural. These groups will initiate movements which, in turn, will be manifest in their effects not only upon the species and the planet but upon individual lives. Their benefit is likely to be expressed in a greater frequency, or proportion, of individuals finding increasing satisfaction and fulfillment in life. [3.]

In this vision of evolutionary change through well-being, Salk is coming very close to Spangler.

This is a simple difference between a person who is inwardly at peace and attuned to a source of strength and power greater than human level problems and one who is attuned to conflict with such problems and consequently to a consciousness of fear and anxiety

8

and limitation. It is also known that people who are undergoing inner emotional stress are more accident prone, another consequence of this simple difference. Yet, it is just this simple difference that may be the key to the separation of the two worlds, not through something exotic, such as a miraculous translation of an elect few into some other plane, but through something as prosaic as people dying in significantly increasing numbers because they cannot live at peace within themselves and with their world nor can they create conditions of harmony. Earth itself, as a physical place, does not need to be cataclysmically altered in order to usher in the New Age.[4.]

If the individual is to survive, he will have to have a life that does more than meet the basic need of his survival. It is one thing to stand with your fellowmen in a subway in Tokyo or New York, and quite another to stand with them singing Handel's *Messiah*. Human evolution is not simply a matter of creating a technology for our survival, or, as many political scientists suggest, building a fresh ethic *for* our technology.[5.] If we envision man as a clumsy beast who has to hurry to catch up with his own stainless steel technology, then we fail to understand that technology and ethics spring from the very depths of culture, and in those depths, only the artist and the prophet can touch the very well-springs of our being.

Culture does not spring forth from institutes financed by the state. Culture bursts forth from the unconscious: it rises from the cthonic powers of the earth and descends from the celestial visitations of the gods. Christian civilization flowed forth from a baptism in a river by a wild man of the desert; Islamic civilization sprang forth from a vision in a cave. You cannot create Christianity out of Newton's *Principia*, but you can create the *Principia* out of Christianity.

First things must come first, and all new cultures begin with the charismatic explosion of myth, of vision, of revelation. The new evolutionary culture that many scientists and scholars are calling for is not going to come from academic conferences, scholarly monographs, or scientific charts and graphs. The humanizing of technology is not going to come from liberal humanism; the ethics for the control of nature, or genetic engineering is not going to be fashioned in committees. Planetary man is not going to solve the problems of postindustrial man, he is going to move out of the culture in which those problems and their solutions exist.

The seventeenth century scientist did not learn how to solve the problems of the sixteenth century alchemist; he learned how to stop looking for the salamander in the flames. Twenty-first century man will not learn how to solve the problems of twentieth century man: he will not learn how to control "the Green Revolution," he will learn how to talk and listen to plants; he will not learn how to control the weather, but to commune with *devas* of the wind; he will not learn how ethically to control the use of psychosurgery and electronic stimulation of the brain, but how to cure through etheric invocation. Planetary man will not learn how to humanize technology by thinking like a machine, he will humanize technology through animism. The new culture is the consummation of all previous cultures, for only the combined energy of our entire cultural history is equal to the new quantum-leap of evolution. Animism *and* electronics is the new landscape of Findhorn: not the regressive infantilism of the drugged commune or the *Psychology Today* Disneyland of biofeedback, positive reinforcement, aversive therapy, psychosurgery, and ESB.

Culture is full of many surprises, because culture is full of the play of opposites. And so there will be scientists and mystics in the New Age. The Establishment tends to see the New Age as an era of full scientific realization with the last atavistic remnants of religion found only in museums. The Counterculture tends to see the New Age as one of full psychic realization with the last atavistic remnants of technology found only in museums.

To look at the American Counterculture today, one would

10

guess from all the interest in yoga, zen, macrobiotics, and sufism, that the East was about to engulf the West. But, as I have argued before, every vanishing cultural form has its most colorful expression at its sunset. In a Hegelian dialectic of *aufheben*, America is swallowing up and absorbing the traditional Eastern techniques of transformation, because only these are strong enough to humanize its technology. In the days before planetization, when civilization was split between East and West, there were basically two cultural directions. The Westerner went outward to level forests, conquer nations, and walk upon the moon: the Easterner went inward and away from the physical into the astral and causal planes. Now, in the case of David Spangler, and others like him at Findhorn, we can glimpse the beginnings of a new level of religious experience, neither Eastern nor Western, but planetary.

In an earlier age, the shaman fell into trance and lost his own consciousness as he was swamped by the unconscious. Later, the yogi learned to expand his consciousness through meditation and self-enhancing rather than self-immolating disciplines. Now prophetic figures like Spangler seem to be coming forth with a new form of consciousness: not an annihilation of sensory experience through yogic *pratyahara*, but an immediate *dhyana* or attunement so that the self becomes *figure* against the *ground* of being in God's consciousness. Here there is no mediumistic trance, no sitting in meditation for twenty years; one returns from the annihilation of all forms to the All annihilating itself into form. The religious discipline for this level of consciousness is not the *sadhu* alone in his cave, but the unique individual living in a universal community in which the group energies create the etheric embodiment of a god. With the fully individual self attuned to God and *devas*, the new man goes forth to act in a new culture in which action is not the negation of consciousness. Through Findhorn and the work of David Spangler, we can glimpse a science fiction landscape of the future in which men and women move among the trees and machines, hearing the dryads in one and the molecular chorus of God in the crystal lattice of the other.

But let us not jump to conclusions and assume that the appearance of a new pattern means the contemptuous rejection of the old. *Aufheben* works through loving incorporation rather than hateful exclusion. The new spirituality does not reject the earlier patterns of the great universal religions. Priest and church, *guru* and *chelas* will not disappear; they will not be forced out of existence in the New Age, they will be absorbed into the existence of the New Age. Nowhere is this pattern more clear than at Findhorn, where yogis and Zen Buddhists, Jews and Protestant ministers sit side by side in the silent meditation of "Sanctuary."

David Spangler and Findhorn are, like Ficino and the Academy of Renaissance Florence, the seeds of a whole new cultural epoch. In this book we can see an entire world view; for many people this new world view will seem most alien. But cultural transformations do not proceed in easy transitions; they move in quantum-leaps, and only a conversion experience or a revelation can give one the energy to leap across the abyss that separates one world view from another. A Roman Senator cannot become a Frankish Christian without first dying and being reborn.

As Spangler's transmission has expressed it, we are already living in two worlds, joined by the potential of a creative synthesis. Perhaps because I still travel back and forth between these two worlds, I would have more people consider Spangler's work, and its visions of rebirth and wholeness. Of all the esoteric thinkers I know, he is the most lucid. He has none of the thaumaturgical obscurantism of the occultist, none of the syrupy sweetness of the blissed-out devotee, and none of the religious pride of the guru. To witness him in transmission is to take part in an overwhelming experience, and yet he is never overwhelmed or unbalanced. Always a sense of whimsy and playfulness returns to remind us that Revelation is not something supernatural and larger than life; it is what life is all about.

1   Teilhard de Chardin, *The Phenomenon of Man* (New York: Harper & Row, 1961), p.30.
2   Jonas Salk, *The Survival of the Wisest* (New York: Harper & Row, 1973), p. 62.
3   Ibid., p.82.
4   David Spangler, pp. 168-69.
5   Daniel Callahan, *The Tyranny of Survival* (New York: Macmillan, 1973).

FOREWORD

by Sir George Trevelyan, Bt., M.A.

Much talk there is of a New Age. Many are filled with a mounting sense of expectation. It was Teilhard de Chardin in the closing pages of *Le Milieu Divin* who wrote that "expectation . . . is perhaps the supreme Christian function and the most distinctive characteristic of our religion. . . . We persist in saying that we keep vigil in expectation of the Master but in reality many would have to admit, if they were sincere, that they no longer expect anything. The flame must be revived at all costs. At all costs we must renew in ourselves the desire and the hope for the Great Coming."

Though ever more people now look to some sort of change, there are many questions in our minds. What is meant by a New Age? Is it coming or has it, somehow, already come? Is it going to happen with a thunderclap or slowly seep into our consciousness? Is it an inner change in individuals or an outer change in circumstances? There is talk of world changes. The mind boggles when it tries to envisage what this could mean. A second coming? Is the Christ to appear again among us and if so, how? Will new avatars and inspired teachers reveal themselves? It is all very exciting and very difficult.

This inspiring book will help many. It contains an interpretation of present circumstances and the events leading up to them which sets the stage for what could be the greatest step in human history and evolution. It is clear to us all that we have to think big. As Christopher Fry wrote:

"Affairs are now soul size.
The enterprise is exploration in to God. . . ."

The adventure is one of expanding consciousness. The landing of men on the moon, though a fantastic achievement of group creative thought, technology, administration and courage, was nevertheless an exploration still within the

15

physical dimension. It becomes clear that a different form of space exploration is possible by crossing the frequency-rates which demarcate different levels of being and thus entering into an expanded dimension of thought. We have to realize that higher worlds are not merely higher in space but are planes of consciousness and "being" existing in a different vibrational band and therefore quite invisible to our five senses and earth-bound consciousness. Nevertheless, human thinking, when strengthened and lifted through meditation, is a universal organ which can blend with the Thinking which is the very stuff of the universe.

The great seers and adepts of our age have shown that it is possible to reunite with the Primal Oneness which, in a condition of absolute being, life and creative thought, underlies all the created world. This amounts to a true form of conscious exploration into further dimensions. It involves indeed a blending of consciousness in heightened awareness with beings from higher planes. This is the new and true *communion* for our age, which carries us beyond the trance mediumship which characterized the earlier generations of spiritualism. Though much was learned through mediums of integrity, the possibility of blending in full consciousness with the thoughts of beings on higher spiritual planes opens the possibility for an undreamt of extension of human knowledge. A veritable new Renaissance could come if this mental communion were truly achieved. There is nothing which could not be done by man in co-operation with higher worlds. Exalted and light-filled beings could work with us, impregnating our consciousness with new knowledge, love and inspiration, and those who have left the body through so-called "death", but are still closely concerned with earth life, could work within our lifted thinking to help us solve the immense problems facing mankind today. With such co-operation, understood as an inner communion in thought and understanding, nothing would be impossible.

This blending of consciousness with higher beings is the new "mediumship" for our time. Perhaps some new world is needed, such as "mediators" or "interpreters", since the extended knowledge is experienced not as coming from some outside source but from within our own thinking and the understanding of the heart.

David Spangler is one who has developed this power and his writing clearly comes from such blending. We can all, however, in our different degrees, begin to work towards this end. It implies that we shall less and less seek guidance from some apparently outside source but shall discover that the spiritual world, once we fully recognize its existence, works with us from within our own thinking, imagination and intuition. Thus, the initial intellectual understanding of the reality of higher worlds and of the primal Divine Unity underlying all diversity leads us first to the longing and need to invoke its help and then to an enrichment of our own consciousness. In this sense we ourselves bring in the New Age from within ourselves.

The thoughts set down in this book are not easy but are of profound relevance for all who are reaching in their minds towards a world-view which goes beyond the materialistic outlook and includes the living Spirit as the power underlying all life. Very difficult concepts are given with a beauty and clarity which will help many to understand the subjective/objective quality of the changes now taking place.

These chapters are by way of being a commentary and expansion on statements given from the higher plane by a Universal Presence identifying Itself archetypally as Limitless Love and Truth. David Spangler is a young American who is devoting his life to teaching and lecturing on New Age themes. He has developed powers of communication through communion with higher worlds and in full consciousness can channel teachings from the spiritual planes. While in Britain and staying at the Findhorn Trust community in Morayshire, Scotland, he received the messages from Limitless Love and Truth, which were subsequently published in separate booklets and pamphlets by the Findhorn Trust and the Universal Foundation. Now he has been inspired to write this commentary, elucidating the difficult meaning of parts of the teaching and placing their significance into an historical, cosmic and personal context.

I recommend all who are interested in the spiritual adventure of modern man to study this book. It gives a broad interpretation which will help many to grasp what may be meant by the New Age, the Cosmic Christ and the Second Coming. There is much joy and a great hope in this writing. David Spangler sees the emergence of a veritable new culture in our time, fired and inspired by living spiritual power but rising from within each soul who can attune to the high vibrations and energies which, as so many believe, have been released into the world. This view, laying the creative responsibility and opportunity on each individual, contains an educational vision of first importance and a challenge which should appeal to modern consciousness. It calls us to lift our hearts toward the New Age, present for discovery in our midst, within ourselves and now.

AUTHOR'S NOTE
The Story Behind This Book

For most of my life I have been conscious of two worlds, two aspects of reality. One is the so-called normal world, revealed to us through our five senses and their technological extensions. The other is a super-sensory reality, a meta-physical world of light and energy and essence, home to Intelligences more evolved than our own in many cases. This might be called a spiritual or even a mystical dimension, entered through intuition, meditation, ESP and states of altered consciousness: a world behind the world known to our physical senses.

This is not an unusual condition. All of us are aware of these two worlds on some level of our beings, often unconsciously, but a great number of people experience this as a conscious awareness. Eastern religions and some branches of Western psychologies (in addition to a Western tradition of mysticism and esotericism) bring the existence of these higher dimensions and of the beings who inhabit them to our attention.

In my own case, the ability to commune between dimensions developed naturally out of a childhood sensitivity and led me as a teenager into exploring the esoteric and mystical traditions more consciously. This in turn resulted in my becoming a lecturer on esoteric themes, with particular reference to the dawning of a New Age in our time, the emergence of a new cycle of human consciousness and experience for which our troubled century was a period of transformation and transition. I had the good fortune to be joined in my work by Myrtle Glines, a woman of deep sensitivity and intuition who was a professional human relations counsellor. Together we developed a program of

19

lectures and workshops integrating the personality and spiritual levels of approach to the challenge of personal and group transformation and creativity.

As a result of our work, we learned of the Findhorn community in northern Scotland. This was a center based on the practical exploration and demonstration of a New Age consciousness, a place of synthesis between humanity and the divinity within nature. We were impressed by rumors and reports we heard about the place, with its magical garden growing on sand due to help from elves, fairies and angelic beings. In the summer of 1970, circumstances unfolded for us to travel to Europe where, according to information I was receiving from higher levels of consciousness, we would find the keys to our next cycle of work. There was nothing given specifically as to just where or when this discovery would be made, and I speculated that it would most likely be in Europe itself. Findhorn was not in my mind as being the place.

As a consequence, Myrtle and I allowed ourselves three days in the midst of our travelling to take the train from London to Inverness and Forres in Scotland, visit Findhorn and return to London. On our arrival, however, we were both astonished to find a developing community where the sense of co-creative contact with other dimensions of life and the presence of a spiritual and integrative energy was stronger than any other place we had ever visited. Furthermore, we found an immediate and deep rapport with Findhorn's founders, Peter and Eileen Caddy and Dorothy Maclean. Long before the three days were up, there was no question in our minds that this was the place where we were to begin our next cycle of work. At the same time, Peter and Eileen had made an unprecedented step of accepting us as co-directors of the center with them. Though we had made no provisions for a lengthy stay in Britain, events fell into place for us to do so; as it turned out, our projected three-day visit became three years before we returned to pick up our work again in the United States.

The summer of 1970 was a crucial time at Findhorn. Up

until then, the community had really been about the size of an extended family, averaging fifteen members. Peter as the central administrator had close, personal contact with each person and provided a powerful energy of inspiration. He shared in all the work and handled many tasks by himself. That summer, however, Findhorn began to expand phenomenally in both population and diversity of activities, going beyond the scope of Peter's personal efforts. There were a few people in the community who constituted something like a "brain trust" and we began meeting to consider this growth. Always, our mental and emotional projections and plans were referred to what could be gained through contact with higher levels.

It was at such a meeting on the 31st of July, 1970, that I became aware on the fringes of my consciousness of a strong presence that was overlighting the proceedings. I shared what I was feeling, and we decided to sit in meditation together and see if this presence could be contacted. I describe the process of this contact in Chapters 3 and 19; the result was communion with an impersonal consciousness that identified itself through the qualities of Limitless Love and Truth. Within that communion, I was able to identify and to communicate the ideas and vision which this presence embodied.

This contact continued off and on through September 3rd, 1970, resulting in seven transmissions in all. Six of them are reproduced here and form the core of this book. The seventh concerned the garden and the relationship with the nature spirits and is printed in a chapter I wrote for *The Findhorn Garden* (Harper & Row, 1975), where its message fits more appropriately into the theme of that book. The other six transmissions all deal with the transition into a New Age, the birth of a new world and a new consciousness, the descent of higher energies of spirit into human consciousness and so forth.

At that time, Findhorn already had a sizeable mailing list of people throughout the world, to whom were distributed a number of publications which the community produced. The six transmissions were transcribed and divided into two booklets which were printed and mailed out to all the Findhorn subscribers. The tapes of the transmissions, particularly of the first two, were played to visitors as well. From this exposure, a number of questions arose. Who or what was Limitless Love and Truth? What were the implications of the two worlds that presence speaks of? What was the larger spiritual context to which these revelations belonged? I decided that another booklet was needed to answer these and other questions and to provide a framework for the transmissions.

When I sat down to write, I envisioned a publication of about twenty to thirty pages. I had no intention of writing a book. However, as I began, it was as if I were overlighted by another aspect of this presence of Limitless Love and Truth. Insights which I had gained over the years through my communions with higher levels, new information, and a deeper identification with some of the processes behind that presence all came together in a synthesis of inspiration, and I found myself writing non-stop for several days. Myrtle and I had a deadline then; we needed to leave Findhorn the first week of November to return to California where we could put our affairs in order to permit us to return and live in the community. It was towards the end of September when I began this project and I knew I had to finish it before we left. I did not bother with drafts. I simply wrote as it flowed within my consciousness, making few changes afterwards. It was two days before our departure date when I finished and discovered that I had a manuscript that exceeded a hundred pages in length.

Throughout that winter while we were in America, the Findhorn publishing team, with a young American named Alexis as the editor-in-chief, worked getting the manuscript ready for printing. The size of the project went beyond Findhorn's capabilities, so a new printing press was ordered and a larger building was converted to house it. In April of

1971, Myrtle and I returned; still the work continued of pasting up, editing, getting the new press in order and people trained to use it, experimenting with ways of binding, collating, printing. Finally, in August, after much work on the part of Victor Bailey, the head of printing and publications for the community, and on the part of many, many other people, the book was completed and sent out to all on the mailing list.

After that, our attention turned to other things: the establishment of the community on a more stable foundation, the development of a performing arts department and of an educational program, and so forth. I forgot about *Revelation*. It had, after all, been written for a very specific audience to fill a specific need. That need had been met; as new visitors arrived and were exposed to the Limitless Love and Truth transmissions, copies of the book were available for sale by the community.

Revelation, however, took on a life of its own. The community kept receiving more requests for it; bookstores began ordering it. Soon it was out of print, and a second printing was run in November of 1971. Groups in Britain and the United States began ordering it in bulk, and one university in New York State ordered a number of copies as a text in a class in modern religious phenomena.

I paid little attention to all this. Myrtle and I were extremely busy with our educational work in the community. Then, in the spring of 1973, we received information from higher levels that we should return to America and take up our work there again. It was after we had returned that I discovered the path which the book had been taking. Everywhere we traveled we met people who had read it, people who knew very little about Findhorn but who had somehow acquired a copy of *Revelation*. Again and again I heard how much the message in the transmissions had meant and how people had felt a power from them.

In all honesty I was embarrassed by this. In the first place, I had tried hard all my life to deglamorize my contact with other levels, to avoid being thought of as a "channel" or a psychic medium. Just as that contact was very normal for me, I felt it important to convey that normalcy and help others find similar attunement within themselves. To be thought of as a prophet or a seer seemed to work against that intention.

Secondly, the book was heavily oriented towards the esoteric and the metaphysical. It was written assuming that its audience already had some familiarity with the concepts of these fields. Now the book was being widely distributed beyond the original audience for which it had been written; consequently, even while being attracted to its theme, individuals were having difficulty understanding it. As someone whose educational philosophy values clear, understandable communication highly, I found this disturbing as well. I also wished I could polish up the writing and expand the subject matter beyond the esoteric themes, since my own work encompasses more than just those themes. I even discovered to my horror that there was a tendency here and there to use the book in a cultish way, as if it were a new gospel.

All of these matters were on my mind when my good friend, Ira Friedlander, editor and publisher for Rainbow Bridge Publications offered to prepare an American edition of *Revelation*. Since the original Findhorn plates were too worn out to be used any more, the entire book would have to be reset, which meant that I could change it in any way I wished. I could, in fact, completely rewrite it, which is exactly what I intended to do.

At the same time, however, I arranged with a Boston publisher, Seymour Lawrence Incorporated, who publish in cooperation with Delacorte and Dell, to do a new book on the idea and the phenomena of a New Age and a transformation in consciousness. Titled *EMERGENCE: Reflections on a New Age and a New Humanity*, this book soon became my main project and an outlet for many of the ideas which I had thought of rewriting into *Revelation*. I also discovered that people were not having as much difficulty with the original book as I had thought, or at least, the challenge of the concepts seemed to be part of its value.

In short, I realized that *Revelation* was all of a piece: transmissions and commentaries all stemmed ultimately from the same source, the same experience and should stand together unchanged. Whatever its strengths or faults, the book itself is a phenomenon, a wholeness. Thus, it is reproduced in this American edition just as it was written in a torrent of inspiration five years ago.

I have, however, made some concessions to a changing consciousness. I have added an introductory first part which I hope will provide a context for understanding and approaching the original material. In it I describe briefly the nature of the esoteric tradition and its approach to reality, the nature of Findhorn and the nature of my attunement to higher levels. I trust this part will be of assistance to those who approach these concepts for the first time and for whom this book may be an initial contact with the idea and vision of a New Age.

In the original book, the transmissions were placed in an appendix, along with an article I had written in conjunction with the first Limitless Love and Truth booklets Findhorn mailed out, "New Age Energies and New Age Laws." Though the latter is not a transmission, I include it again since it was composed under the same flow of inspiration. In this edition, the transmissions make up Part II, while the bulk of the manuscript, the commentaries and interpretations, are Part III.

Part IV contains a new transmission from Limitless Love and Truth received January 8, 1975. It forms an important part of the whole, as does the accompanying message from "John", a presence I often work with on higher levels. It also contains some thoughts concerning the process of revelation five years after the first transmissions and concerning the birth of a new age. It shows, I trust, that there is no end to revelation; it is an on-going process for each of us, for it is born of life and its will to grow and to become. Its purpose is to open the vision out for each of us, so that the power and presence of revelation, of Limitless Love and Truth will not end when you close the covers of this book.

David Spangler
Belmont, California, USA
August, 1975

Part I
Introduction to Revelation

Chapter 1

Revelation and Reality

Solar Logos, Earth Logos, Cosmic Consciousness, The New Age, the Cosmic Christ, Light, Energy, the Etheric Plane . . . these words may be new and strange to you, the concepts behind them even stranger. They embody a particular way of looking at the world, a way often labelled "mystical", "esoteric" or even "occult". They seem to have little relationship to "hard" reality: the world of business, science and politics, of work, family and the personal quest for security and happiness. On the other hand, words like *mitochondria, deoxyribonucleic acid, quantum, quark, ion, cybernetics* and *complementarity* are every bit as strange, describing processes, laws, elements and substances which most people do not directly encounter in the course of daily reality and of which they may be quite unfamiliar. Yet, all of reality as we know it depends on the existence and functioning (often on levels beyond our ability to perceive or describe except mathematically) of those things these words represent.

The mystic, the physicist, the economist, the biologist, the engineer, the constructor, the policeman, the psychologist, the politician, the lawyer — in fact, every type of worker and professional — evolves a language to describe that aspect of reality with which he must deal. In time this language, the jargon of the trade, becomes incomprehensible to an outsider, and a breed of interpreters develops to enable different disciplines and professions to communicate with each other. At first, the words and concepts of an international economist, a logician, an art critic or a political strategist may be as esoteric to me as my own area of experience in transpersonal psychologies may be to them. Yet, a willingness to openly appraise and understand such specialized languages within the context of the discipline or work they represent usually reveals a logic and a pattern that is easily comprehensible. I can enter into another's reality system and understand it, but first I must overcome my attachment to the familiar or my antipathy to what is new and strange.

We speak of "hard" reality as if it were something fixed and solid for all time and for all people. Yet, what is hard reality for the molecular biologist, the quantum theorist, the mathematician, chemist or nuclear physicist may be the height of abstraction and even fantasy for a farm laborer, a struggling small business owner or a clerk, until they learn to appreciate each other's languages and the aspect of reality which they are trying to describe. Likewise, reality is different for the corporate executive, the ghetto welfare mother, the Soviet commissar, the Arab oil shiek, the tribesman of central Africa, the yogi of India. Humanity is fragmented into different cultural, economic, political, religious and climatic worlds. Furthermore, our ideas of reality change through time. The reality of late twentieth century humanity in the industrialized countries is not that of medieval Europe or Asia; it is not even that of the nineteenth century. Only a hundred years ago, scientists were writing that we had discovered almost everything there was to know about the universe; the atomistic, mechanistic view prevailed: creation was a vast machine governed by Newton's laws of motion. The revolution wrought by quantum theory, relativity theory, the atom bomb, and new discoveries in astronomy changed all that. Matter is no longer solid; it is energy in motion, crystallized vibrations: the most fundamental units of existence turn out to be mathematical processes and probabilities rather than actual, substantial things. The universe is ultimately the manifestation of non-physical, non-material possibilities, and the dominant view of science now is how much we don't really know about the nature of reality.

This is not always a comfortable viewpoint. We are happier when we feel we are in control through possession of relevant knowledge and skills. To admit how much we don't know is to challenge the security of that control. It is to affirm our vulnerability before the universe. Of course, this can be an opportunity to open ourselves to growing into deeper and broader relationships with our universe, but all too often, we are not seeking an open-ended process of blending with life but some platform or vantage point of knowing where we can stand unthreatened and in control, like a military commander always seeking the ideal terrain, the highest point, on which to construct his defenses. If security means the ability to hold on to what we have and to what we think we are, then we use knowledge and our interpretations of reality to give us that. We seek learning and growth in order to overcome the insecurity of ignorance rather than to gain a more dynamic security of wisdom and continual movement with life through changing vistas of reality.

Reality changes because we change in our perceptions and experiences of it. To try and stop that flow is to deny our very life force, our humanity. It is to try to force limitless truth into a particular container of information and say that it is the whole of truth. This is manifestly a futile task whose only result is continual conflict between the various containers that men devise and between the containers and the limitless content beyond.

The esoteric disciplines represent a container which various individuals and groups have developed over the millenia to capture and study for a moment the ceaseless dynamics of a living universe. I should say "containers", since these disciplines are as varied as human cultures, while the esoteric tradition is really many sub-traditions or factions. At its highest, this tradition (as manifested through its diverse parts) embodies a very penetrating and evolutionary relationship with reality; all that we consider the best in our cultures, the highest in science, art, religion, social consciousness, had its beginning in what were considered at one time (and might still be) esoteric doctrines and studies. On the other hand, like any other branch of human activity and knowledge, when it is subverted to a desire for security and control, it can become a path of orthodoxy or of escape from broader dealings with reality every bit as binding as any ideology that would set itself

31

up as the arbiter of Truth or as any materialist's quest for pleasure and possessions.

The word "esoteric" itself means simply knowledge that is possessed or understood only by a few. In this sense, of course, nearly every branch of knowledge could be considered esoteric with respect to the proportion of the population that is not involved with that branch, as we have discussed. However, even though we may talk about the esoteric nature of physics, international economics or modern communications technology, for example, it is in connection with that tradition of research and insight into the spirit and essence of the universe behind its visible forms that the word is most often used. Esotericism is generally understood as the study of the inner world, the world of the psyche, of the spirit, of the invisible processes which give rise to outer reality. It is the world of the mystic, the occultist, the psychic, the parapsychologist, the guru, the adept, the practitioner of arcane magical arts, the theosophist.

There is a certain glamor that surrounds the esoteric tradition. It has a reputation for exotic beliefs, strange practices, magical powers. It attracts many because of that glamor and because they believe that truth can only be found beyond the realms of form and matter. It likewise repells many as being superstitious nonsense, a trap for the credulous, an escape from the real world (as they interpret it), or at best as being too subjective an approach, lacking the safeguards of impersonal, objective science and therefore being too open to personal imagination and bias to really give firm data about reality. It may be all right for evolving a personal philosophy and sense of values but not for describing the nature of things.

The point I seek to make is that neither of these points of view really embraces the nature and potential of the esoteric tradition. It is neither the one and only True way of looking at things, as some would have it, nor is it fantastic delusion practiced by charlatans. It is simply one container that we have discovered to catch the outpouring of reality. It is undoubtedly more useful than some containers in certain situations and not so useful in others, but no container, no discipline or branch of learning and activity should be expected to catch all of a limitless truth, nor should any container be scorned out of hand as being too leaky to catch any.

Esoterics is simply a language and a set of concepts developed to describe ourselves and our relationship to the greater whole of the universe. If approached in this manner, it can be used as successfully as many other such languages. It can be argued it is not as objective as, say, the language of physics, but this is to misunderstand the nature of modern physics, which, by comparison to classical Newtonian physics of a hundred years ago, is downright mystical. One of the aspects of the revolution of quantum mechanics, as expressed in Heisenberg's Uncertainty Principle, is the demolishing of the myth of the impersonal, objective scientific observer. Every scientist brings a certain bias to his work; furthermore, the very act of observing on a subnuclear level alters that which is being observed. Observer and observed are one, which is a thought long held and taught by many esoteric spiritual traditions. We are not observing Reality with a capital "R", hard and fixed, but we are observing that reality which is revealed or created by the act and quality of our observation. We cannot determine the position of an electron, for example, as I might perceive the position of my lamp on my desk; I can only say statistically that this is where it probably is as influenced by the very act of my perceiving it through my instrumentation. There is a principle of uncertainty built in due to the interaction and effect of the observer and the mechanisms of observation on what is being seen.

On the atomic and subatomic or quantum level, reality is a joint creation or product of the participation of observer and observed. Some thinkers in modern physics are exploring the inference that this is so on the gross level of tables, chairs, desks, lamps and persons as well: our act of perception changes what we see and in turn changes us; reality is continually co-created. While it is interesting that the thoughts of scientists are being led in this direction, this idea of an interrelated, co-creating participatory reality is one that has often been experienced and described in mystical and esoteric literature.

Another and related viewpoint of reality that is now being considered scientifically but which is right out of the esoteric tradition is the role that belief and desire play in perception. There is considerable research indicating that we perceive only what we think or believe we can perceive; that is, whatever our understanding of reality is, our perceptions are selectively censored by our unconscious minds to fit and support that understanding. We create the world we experience through our thoughts, which filter out everything else that is extraneous or that threatens the security of our world view, except when circumstances or a willingness to grow bypass those filters. The only thing that is "hard" about reality is the fixity or the tenacity with which we may hold to certain interpretations and preconceptions about the way things are, becoming an opinionated stone in the midst of the currents of life. The world is as hard as we wish it to be, or as open, fluid and expanding as we can embody.

Much more could be discussed on this subject of reality and the ways in which we perceive and/or create it. If you are interested, I have listed a number of books in the Suggested Reading List in the appendix. Works such as Carlos Castenanda's tales of Don Juan, Joseph Chilton Pearce's *The Crack in the Cosmic Egg* and *Exploring the Crack in the Cosmic Egg*, and *Other Worlds, Other Universes: Playing the Reality Game*, edited by Brad Steiger and John White all deal with the vastness and mutability of reality. For a discussion of the myth of the unbiased, wholly objective observer in science and research, Thomas Kuhn's book, *The Structure of Scientific Revolutions*, is excellent. The manner in which belief and preconceptions affect perception is dealt with in *The Psychology of Consciousness* by Robert Ornstein. Finally, Lawrence LeShan's *The Medium, the Mystic, and the Physicist* and Fritjof Capra's *The Tao of Physics* explore the similarities and the increasing convergence between physical science and the esoteric and mystical world views.

To return to our definition of esoterics, as a philosophy of the inner quest for spiritual understanding and power, it has taken many forms. To simplify matters, however, let us define it as the study of reality from the standpoint of consciousness and the non-material processes of creation. It is the study of the spirit and the essence behind the world of phenomena and material form. Much of the esoteric tradition, both ancient and modern, deals basically with matters of psychology. Other parts, though, deal with the rhythms, the processes, the forces, principles and laws which govern and mold the unfoldment of the universe. Perhaps the basic tenet common to almost all forms of esoteric and mystical thought is that these processes and laws are all the expression of a single Life; that the universe is, therefore, a wholeness, a oneness; and that this wholeness is permeated by a governing quality to which we give the labels of mind, intelligence or consciousness. At every level of manifestation this one Life and consciousness is focused through appropriate, interrelated Beings who can embody it. Thus, the universe is a community of many Life forms which all exist in a dynamic, co-creative communion of the One Life.

Using this definition, *Revelation* is a look at the phenomena of transformation occuring upon our world at this time from the standpoint of consciousness and the dynamics of a spiritual universe. It considers the birth of a new age. Now, there are many reasons why, in looking upon our societies, we might perceive a new age emerging: technological progress, planetary politics and economics, dwindling resources demanding changes in lifestyles, new insights into science and human consciousness, and so forth. In this book, we are looking at this emergence from the inside out, saying that, while all these outer factors exist, there are also inner factors of growth and evolution which are promoting the birth of a new world. With a holistic viewpoint that perceives Life in all things, these internal factors of evolution spring not only from

35

within you and me as individuals, or from within humanity as a species, but from within the earth as an organism in itself (called in esoteric language the "Earth Logos") and in an interrelated way, from within the solar system as a still vaster organism.

It is this perspective of seeing life, intelligence and vital growth within all things, even within seemingly inanimate matter, that may seem most strange about the reality view of *Revelation* and the esoteric tradition. However, it is this very view that is being substantiated by the convergence of science with this tradition. Furthermore, we are semantically constrained by a too-narrow definition of life and intelligence. Mind and intelligence, even life, as we know it as human beings may be only a reflection, a subset, of a much greater universal principle of organization, actualization and co-creative interaction. What we call life and intelligence may seem as inert and inanimate, as dull and inchoate when compared to that principle as a rock may seem to us.

Again, it is our beliefs and preconceptions that may blind us to fuller aspects of reality. One of the functions of the esoteric tradition, of myth and mysticism is to challenge that blindness, to awaken us to a broader outlook with the expectation that such an awakening will give us greater power to positively, creatively and harmoniously interact with reality. This does not always happen. We may try to simply exchange "containers" and make the esoteric viewpoint "THE" Reality, rather than using it in a complimentary way with other, more material viewpoints to gain a more holistic and integrative insight. At this stage in our affairs as a species, when we are faced with truly planetary crises such as pollution, overpopulation, the threat of nuclear war and so forth, we must seek out new planetary perspectives equal to the task of survival and growth. We cannot afford to be blinded in any way or bound to limited ways of looking at reality which cannot open us to the possibilities, the wholeness and the powers of synthesis that we need.

We live in a strange time. We are either afraid of the

transcendental, the mystical, the sublime within ourselves and within our world, denying its existence or importance in the scheme of things; or we swing to the other extreme, becoming too irrational, too mystical, too given to the pursuit of elusive occult powers and knowledge, yearning for some messiah to supernaturally deal with our problems. Between these extremes, however, revelation is taking place in many areas of human endeavor. A new consciousness of reality, a new image of humanity and of the universe is taking shape in our midst.

This book is born out of this tide of revelation and new insight that is sweeping through all human affairs. Its "esoteric" approach makes it neither closer to nor farther from the truth, neither more or less fantastic than the discoveries of modern physics, genetics or parapsychology. This approach simply represents the best way at this time to express certain ideas, certain perspectives about the world we live in and the growth which it is experiencing — perspectives, I feel, which are very significant and helpful and not always found in other approaches. It asks us to consider ourselves in a co-creative relationship with cosmic forces of Life and Beingness. It suggests that we can be points of living focus for a love that is limitless and that is the soul of all that is, the communion that makes the universe a oneness, and that we can experience a reality that is limitless in the truth of its nature, inviting us to grow and expand into its infinite potentialities. By being these things, we become living revelations and the co-creators of a new world, participants in the birth of a New Age.

Chapter 2
Findhorn and Revelation

The theme of this book is the birth of a New Age. This birth is produced by the emergence within humanity (as the species with the greatest self-consciousness) of a new consciousness of itself and of its world. Such a revisioning of reality reveals new possibilities of perception, awareness, behavior and creativity, which, when acted upon with skill and wisdom, can create the forms of a new planetary civilization. The question, of course, is just what is the nature of this new consciousness. What are the forms that it will create?

Many individuals and groups throughout the world are exploring and trying to answer these questions. Some are doing so along traditional lines of research and extrapolation of current trends; the art and science of futurology is a growing one, with numerous conferences occuring every year for its practitioners within the fields of government, science, social studies, and business. Others are trying to describe the features of a changing society through parapsychological, intuitive, and spiritual means. They seek to open themselves to inspiration by an embodiment of the forces of the future acting within the world, like the life forces acting within a seed to direct its growth, trusting that the "spirit of the New Age" will guide them in its externalization. Often these people, who make up what could loosely be called a "New Age movement," are becoming seed-people, experiencing in their lives the revisioning which more academic approaches are trying to research and describe in the jargon of the social planners and designers. However, all approaches to the future are potentially obscured and influenced by the momentum and conditioning of the past and present, the forces of habit, inertia, crystallization, vested interest, attachment to the familiar and so forth. To the extent that our minds are caught in the web of past creations, they are not reliable instruments for this revisioning. The route to the new, then, might not be through following a mental blueprint, which may retain too many features of older, unwanted structures or which may create unnecessary conflict by rejecting a pattern simply because it is old and time-tested. It may be through an organic unfoldment stimulated by a personal, living commitment to growth and openness. It may come not by planning for a New Age and trying to make it happen but by giving it the internal and external space to allow the birth to take place.

This is the philosophy behind the Findhorn Foundation community in northern Scotland. Here is a place where a group of people are seeking to relate to each other and to their world in such a way that if a New Age is seeking to be born, a new consciousness trying to emerge, it will have an opportunity to do so. The results have been remarkable in several ways, bringing Findhorn to the attention of the world as a seedcenter where the qualities and forms of a new culture may indeed be sprouting from the dark soil of the future.

As I mentioned in my Note at the beginning of this book, Myrtle Glines and I became deeply associated with Findhorn beginning in the summer of 1970, and it was there that these transmissions from Limitless Love and Truth took place and the original manuscript of *Revelation* was written. In its original editions, this book went to people who were already familiar with this center; in preparing it for a wider audience, I feel some introduction and description of Findhorn is important.

Findhorn is the name of a river that winds its way through the fertile Scottish lowlands, through the ancient burgh of Forres and down to the Moray Firth, a large bay five miles away opening into the North Sea. Where the river meets the Firth, the smaller Findhorn Bay is created, forming a peninsula at the tip of which is an old fishing village, named, appropriately enough, Findhorn village. The waters around Findhorn are warmed by the proximity of the Gulf Stream, favored by long stretches of beaches and an abnormal amount of sunshine and clear days. As a consequence, the peninsula is a favorite vacation spot for the industrial workers and the clerks of Glasgow and Edinburgh in the summer; to house these visitors, trailer parks have developed in the area.

In the fall of 1962, Peter and Eileen Caddy, their three sons and Dorothy Maclean, a friend and co-worker, were forced by a chain of circumstances to settle in a trailer in one of these parks. Unlike the summer parks that only stayed open a few months of the year, this one, the Findhorn Bay Caravan Park, was the winter home of a number of Royal Air Force personnel stationed at the adjacent RAF base of Kinloss. Peter had just been relieved of his position as manager of a large hotel in nearby Forres and now faced the prospect of spending the winter in a trailer or caravan, living on welfare unless he could find new employment. With his successful career as an RAF officer and a hotel executive, he felt that wouldn't be difficult. As it turned out, however, every job offer he investigated fell through.

To supplement their income, they decided to grow a garden, something none of them had done before. Against them was the state of the terrain: they were living on a beach with very little topsoil, and what there was of it was very deficient in essential nutrients. Mostly, there was just sand. The winds frequently blew with gale force in from the North Sea, their salt content further drying things out.

They did, however, have some unusual factors working for them. Peter, Eileen, and Dorothy had all had unusual backgrounds, giving them great perseverance and faith. Each of them had experienced intense spiritual disciplines and an inner life of contact with God. Eileen and Dorothy, in fact, had developed a capacity to go into silent meditation and receive communications from a source identifying itself as "the God within". It was through such communications that their decision to create a garden was confirmed and they were told they would be given the help they would need to meet the challenges of their environment.

This help came from an unexpected quarter. While in meditation one day, Dorothy was told that behind all the forces and forms of nature there were invisible Beings of great power and intelligence. These Beings, called *Devas* from the Sanskrit meaning "Shining Ones", embodied the energies of growth, life and formation; each species of plant was represented by a Deva, while there were also Devas of mountains, seas, of geographical locations, of natural forces such as wind and rain and of qualities such as sound and color. She was asked to contact the Devas behind the plant species they were trying to grow, and through that contact, they would receive assistance in the garden.

Dorothy found that she could make contact with these Beings. From them, she would relay to Peter information such as how to plant certain seeds, how much water to give, how to make compost and so on; more importantly, they began receiving insights into the relationship between man and his world, between the thoughts and feelings of individuals and the environment. They were told that the quality of their consciousness, the energies of mind and heart which they emitted, was a most important factor in the health and vitality of the garden.

By acting on these instructions and by learning to harmonize themselves psychologically and spiritually with the forces of the garden, miracles began to happen. The story of this garden and of the work with the nature forces is well told in *The Findhorn Garden*, published by Harper and Row and written by several members of the community. (As I mentioned in my Note, it also contains one of the Limitless Love and Truth transmissions concerning humanity's relationship with nature.) Suffice it to say here that the garden flourished and in time became a source of attraction to many people from Britain and other parts of the world. When some of these people decided to stay and participate in this experiment, the Findhorn community began to develop.

For seven years this development was slow and steady. In Peter's words, they were "laying the foundations" for what was to come. The garden provided the main focus of activity, and the yoga of the group was work. It was not a center for philosophizing or discussion. "Work," said Eileen's guidance, "is love in action," and love was very active, indeed. The demands of the garden, of laying plumbing and preparing sites for new caravans and bungalows, of construction and other activities kept the small community of about a dozen people busy from dawn till dusk, and often into the night.

When Myrtle and I arrived, this rhythm was beginning to expand. More people were arriving and settling in trailers. A number of these were artists, who brought a whole different flavor into the work program and life of the center. More young people arrived, and as many of them had little or no previous contact with the esoteric teachings on which Findhorn was based, there was a need to share and discuss these matters. Because of our work as lecturers and counsellors, Myrtle and I injected a definite educational, philosophical and human relations note into the proceedings, which by that time was just what was needed. Findhorn was growing up rapidly on the strong foundations that had been layed. It was beginning to see itself as a place not just of preparation for some future New Age but as a center of emergence of a new vision and consciousness that could make that New Age possible. It needed to make its inherent philosophy and vision more explicit.

The bedrock of Findhorn's development had been Peter, Eileen and Dorothy's attunement to Divinity. They each experienced contact with a God-source within themselves; though this was different for each of them, it was complementary, and they followed the directions they received implicitly. Findhorn was a God-centered community, a theocracy for which Eileen's guidance was the ultimate source of direction. After some time had passed, they were guided to collect and print some of the messages she had received and make them available. They were assisted in this project (and given a large mailing list for the initial distribution) by a group headquartered in England. This group had developed around a series of prophecies made by an invisible spiritual Being known as the All-Knowing One. Depicted as an archetypal, Christ-like figure, the source of these prophecies, which

42

concerned the beginning of a New Age, was also known as Limitless Love and Truth. Many of the supporters of this group also became supporters of Findhorn as booklets containing Eileen's messages went out to them and they became aware of the community.

When I contacted a presence of considerable power and universality on July 31st, 1970 during a planning meeting at Findhorn, it was as if these various elements all came together. The message of this presence concerned the birth of a New Age and Findhorn's role in it; it provided a vision for the community as it prepared to take a new step in its growth, and it provided a universal vision as well. I was aware that this Presence also wished to be identified as Limitless Love and Truth, although I had no direct contact with the other group which had also been in contact with a similar presence. There seemed to be three reasons for this: first, Limitless Love and Truth described the essential qualities of this presence and its message. Secondly, it was an identification that would link immediately and easily with Findhorn's history and be recognized by many of its supporters. Thirdly, it was an attempt to proclaim the universal nature of that presence and counteract a tendency to develop a cult around the previous Limitless Love and Truth phenomena that would have limited its message to a particular group or place. (The original group that had gathered about the prophecies of the All-Knowing One had largely dispersed but there were tendencies to transform what was left into a specific organization and set of teachings, making the image of Limitless Love and Truth into that of a teacher and source for that organization rather than that of a universal presence.)

These transmissions played an important part in the development of Findhorn after 1970. On the other hand, the work and life of the community, what it is demonstrating, provides substance and foundation for the transmissions. Findhorn and the Limitless Love and Truth transmissions received in 1970 are intimately related, each reflecting the other, for both are reflections of the phenomenon of emergence and transformation making our time one of the most important of human history. Both stem from the impulse to revision reality and to gain a deeper attunement to ourselves, to each other and to our world. Both are revelation in action.

The transmissions speak of co-creating a new world by being Limitless Love and Truth in action, by living the Life of that presence. Findhorn is a demonstration of what living that Life may mean. Undoubtedly that demonstration will become clearer and more precise as time goes along, but in the meantime, it is already throwing some illumination on what the new consciousness may be like.

It requires a broader grasp of the meaning of life, a new animism that can relate to levels of intelligence and being beyond the human, beyond the material. It is a consciousness of communion and of community, of working together with each other and with nature to build a world. It is a consciousness of synergy, which is the principle of the part and the whole serving each other, where the whole is greater than the sum of its parts but where neither the part nor the whole grows or expresses to the disadvantage of the other. It is a consciousness attuned to the laws of organic expression, attuned to the nature behind nature, the processes and rhythms of being. It goes beyond the mind and the feelings, yet includes these in a more fulfilled way. It works with the existence of spiritual dimensions, not through worship and awe but through understanding and co-creativity. It does not deny the physical world nor the body but sees them as part of the holistic nature of the universe and seeks to "bring heaven down to earth." In its quest for synthesis and wholeness, this consciousness is neither "airy-fairy" nor "nitty-gritty". If anything, it is "airy-gritty". It is a consciousness of oneness and of the world that can be built to demonstrate oneness.

Perhaps most importantly, the message both of Limitless Love and Truth and of Findhorn is that the New Age is here now. It is a spirit within us, a vision, a seed, a presence that is beyond time and able to enter us now if we will permit it. This orientation gives Findhorn a tremendous creative power and atmosphere. It is not waiting for a New Age; it is building it now.

Of course, in any pioneering effort, there can be errors. Findhorn has its challenges, and while it is easy to glamorize the place, to do so pays it a disservice. It is composed of an ever-changing population of individuals who represent a cross-section of most any American or European town. They are of all ages, religious backgrounds, educational accomplishments and represent several nationalities. They have their challenges together, their joys, sorrows, mistakes and victories. But through it all is this vision of the potentials of humanity and of the earth, the vision of oneness, of wholeness, of being co-creators. The community is trying to make that vision real, and sometimes in the confrontation with older habits and ways of viewing reality, pain results. Findhorn does not have all the answers. It does, however, have a spirit of making revelation come alive and of making the promise of Limitless Love and Truth come alive for a hungry world.

Chapter 3

Identity and Communion

Findhorn, its vision of a holistic world and its dedication to the service of co-creating a new culture was the setting for the Limitless Love and Truth transmissions. Most of the transmissions took place within a small group of people; others took place in the presence of the whole community, which at that time numbered about thirty people including some summer visitors. What was the process by which this communication was created?

Since I was a young child, I have had experiences of contact with other dimensions of reality besides the physical one. Often these were the kind of psychic experiences that most everyone has at some time or another, especially children. Occasionally, they were more than that, becoming experiences of a deep mystical nature. I could not will these to happen (nor did I have any particular desire to as a child); when they did, it was as if my identity as David Spangler would expand beyond its limits, thereby dissolving, and I would be identified with a presence of wholeness beyond the forms of time and space.

While I was in college, I discovered that the natural process of mental expansion due to the intellectual exercise of my studies was bringing my conscious mind into a new and clearer alignment with this other, more transcendental process. Over a period of time, I realized I could become inwardly still and establish a flow of communication with a different level of my identity. In the jargon of the esoteric tradition, I called this my Higher Self.

Through this more precise contact, I began to inwardly discern processes taking place within our world of a transformative nature and became aware of a planetary presence, a new consciousness or life-energy, a spirit of a new age, seeking to externalize itself through humanity. As I mentioned in the Author's Note, this led to my becoming a lecturer on these themes, leaving college and joining Myrtle

Glines, who was a good friend of our family. I was twenty at the time and very uncertain about what the future held, having little more direction than to share what I was experiencing about the dawning of a New Age. Myrtle, on the other hand, was a professional human relations counsellor and an accomplished lecturer. Her own sensitivity and intuitive nature had eventually led her into exploring the esoteric tradition; my need to interpret and communicate what I was inwardly perceiving led me into the field of human communication and practical psychology. Our mutual quests meshed and we began working together: she wished to expand the realm of her service to include what I knew and I wished to be more grounded in her field of wisdom and experience. As we were both seeking new directions in our lives under the prodding of inner guidance, this partnership seemed to provide a practical framework of service in which that direction could emerge. Further, the difference in our ages enabled us to reach together in a broader spectrum of people than we might have done otherwise.

I should say at this point that I have never felt comfortable being identified as a psychic. As I was becoming more aware of my ability to commune with other levels of consciousness, I experienced this as a natural unfoldment and resisted attempts to label it as something exotic or unnatural. During that period, I knew several individuals who were trance mediums, persons who could go into a sleep-like state or trance and allow another individuality to use their bodies to speak through. While respecting these persons and the work they were trying to do, I had no desire to follow that path. I felt intuitively that whatever I was in contact with, I participated in the communication, and the result was a product of both my consciousness and a higher one. I disliked the idea of being a "channel", a passive tube through which some other intelligence would speak, and felt that such communication was not the pattern for the future. I resisted any kind of work or phenomenon that might place me into a position of being considered a "channel".

47

When Myrtle and I began working together, it was with a deep sense of trust in each other and attunement together. Our thoughts and feelings resonated in such a manner that we could work like one being. Not long after we had begun working together, we were sitting in the living room of a friend when I felt like a strong presence had walked into the room. We were alone on a physical level, but I knew someone had entered. On impulse, I reached over and held Myrtle's hand. Almost immediately, I felt my identity being pulled away from its focus on myself and into communion with this presence. While remaining fully conscious and aware, I was immersed in a process of exchanging energy with this Being and entering into its consciousness. As this happened, I felt a flow of impressions and words which I wished to share with Myrtle. It was as if my body was now the focus for an identity that was the joint creation of Myrtle's energy, my own and that of this Being. Eyes closed to maintain my inward concentration, I began to talk as if I were that identity, thus expressing outwardly at least that function and appearance of being a channel that I had long resisted.

This Being said that we could call him "John"; although that was not his name, it was as good as any to help us in conversing with him. He said that he represented a blending of our two High Selves or greater identities and would act as our mentor in our work.

That was in the summer of 1965. Everyday thereafter for nearly a year, we would sit in meditation, and John would blend with us. Although it put me in the position of seeming to be a channel, I knew that there was a reason for it and that I should accept it. If it had not been for Myrtle's trust and confidence in the process, I doubt that I would have been so open to it. It did, however, teach me more understanding and tolerance for those who are truly channels, and it did train me in that process which I call attunement, as described in Chapter 19 and mentioned by Sir George Trevelyan in his Forward. By the time we arrived at Findhorn, I was very comfortable with this process and was able, therefore, to co-communicate the messages of Limitless Love and Truth.

As I mention in Chapter 19, the image of a channel or of much in the way of psychic communication maintains the separation between the communicator and the receiver or transmitter. What I experience is based on the idea of wholeness and oneness, and of communion of identities. This is the nature of ordinary conversation, anyway; rarely are we passive listeners. The meaning of any communication is jointly created by the intent and communicative skills of the speaker and the prejudices, expectations, listening skills, beliefs and ideas of the receiver. Often, we hear only what we want to hear or misinterpret because of semantic differences between us.

The process by which these transmissions are received is an extension of this. It is an empathtic process, a deeper version of the kind of active listening and open participation that marks any good communication between persons. It is based on my conception of identity as being a spectrum along which our attention can move, like a bow moving along a violin and producing different notes. For many of us, we move only within that part of the spectrum as represented by our bodies and the social conditioning that determines our roles. We identify ourselves by our work, our families, our hobbies, our physical forms; yet, inwardly, we know that there is more to us than just what these forms represent.

My experience is that there is an essential Identity within us each, which in turn resonates with and is part of an essential Identity within the universe. Some might call this God, within us and within our world. This essence can be focused, and the lesson of individuality is to learn how to skillfully exercise such a focus: how to be a unique, discrete entity. This essence can also be expanded, and this is the lesson of universality, of coming into resonance with the world about us and transcending our focussed selves. In my case, I experienced this transcendence at an early age and came to accept it as a normal part of identity. However, through meditation and consideration of who one really is apart from particular forms and roles, anyone can come to realize the possibilities of identity on more expanded levels of the spectrum. This, in fact, is the area of research and practice for transpersonal psychology.

To execute this expansion properly, however, I find that it is vital to know and understand the nature of one's focussed self, one's personality. Too often in the metaphysical and esoteric fields and within the New Age movements, I have discovered people who want nothing to do with the "personality level" and the field of human relationships, the politics of living; instead, they want "higher consciousness", "cosmic consciousness", "God consciousness". These are only other parts of the spectrum or scale of our Identity and each part reflects the other. The key to proper communion or attunement, I find, is not to seek one part of the spectrum above another part but to blend with the essence of the spectrum itself. In my own training, the insights that Myrtle could provide into the working of my personality and the personality of persons in general provided an invaluable tool for evaluating and working with information that I would receive.

I am I. This should be obvious. I am neither a personality nor a High Self. I am what I am. In communicating with another, I blend what I am with what the other is, and that oneness is the true communication. To understand that communication, to evaluate it, to even participate in it creatively, I have to know and understand myself. I need to know how I as a vehicle of communication, as a system of information, am most likely to fulfill the process of communication itself.

Thus, in this process of communion with other levels, I never try to lose myself. Rather, I seek a level of openness that allows me to extend myself and come into attunement with whatever other level of consciousness I am seeking to contact. In principle, as I have said, this is no different than the process of any good communication with another.

We communicate best with what we can identify with. As we release our focus upon our particular selves, we discover that the possible range of our communication expands. We discover oneness, the communion of identities. For me, this is an active, conscious, fully participatory process. The resulting communication, whether with John, Limitless Love and Truth or whatever, is a blending of several energies: my consciousness as it spreads along a spectrum of identity, the level and identities with which I am communing, the energies of the environment and of any other people who are present, and the timing and conditions of that moment. This blending is focused through a composite "entity" which is the communication itself, the words, tone, subject matter, place and so forth. As Mcluhan says, "the medium is the message." The oneness is the communication.

Thus, I can transmit the message of Limitless Love and Truth only to the degree that I can be Limitless Love and Truth, identifying with that essence, not just in the moment of communication but as consistently as possible. For communion is based on identity, and our identification with the qualities we would contact on higher levels must be exercised and integrated within ourselves so that we become that with which we would communicate. In this fashion, the process is a never-ending one, and a transmission is only the appearance in a particular time and place of an on-going process.

This is why, for me, it is silly and dangerous to stop the process by placing too much emphasis upon a transmission or by treating it as anything more than a signpost to the process itself. We must live our identities and our communications; they are not events captured in time like a fossel in amber. We are the messages of our lives, not our words. These transmissions suggest a vision and a power that can help us, but there is more to that vision, much more to that power than this or any other book can capture. Revelation goes on; Limitless Love and Truth is always transmitting to and through us, if we can awaken to it. We live in an ocean of communication, filtering most of it away and leaving only that which fits the limits of our accepted identities. Love is limitless; truth is limitless; we are limitless, as well as having

51

the power to focus to meet the requirements of form. Like many sub-nuclear phenomena, we are both an infinite wave and a unique particle; we are the whole and the part, the One and the Individual. Most importantly, we are the capacity to synthesize and commune between these extremes. This is the true power of identity within us, and it is on this power that our ability to communicate rests, as well as our ability to be creators of the new world we would build, the world we sense in the heights of our dreams and at the heart of our communing.

Part II
The Transmissions of Limitless Love and Truth

Chapter 4

First Communication

July 31st 1970

I am Limitless Love and I am one of the sponsors of the unfoldment of this center.

Findhorn is a direct sequence of revelation continuing from my pattern and other patterns around the world constituting a direct link to the spheres of limitless light and love. The energies consecrated into one form are now consecrated into a group action. Findhorn is serving several functions. It serves as a hub from which energies can radiate for the assistance and nourishment of other centers and groups throughout the world. It is building as an etheric center within the body of earth and represents one of the sacred centers of that spiritual planet now touching down and attempting to externalize itself. This is not due so much to this locality, though this is important; it is due to the concentration of energy focussed here, invited here and coming from many sources, all being placed into a reservoir of Light which therefore creates a vehicle for the expression of one of the sacred centers of this earth. It acts as a womb in which seeds can be placed, nourished and unfolded.

Because of your activity in the physical realm, your aspirations, your obedience to the Light you pour forth, it has enabled the creation of an etheric center which is accomplishing a work not fully revealed to you because you have not evolved physical counterparts for it. What appears on the surface as a small but growing community is becoming, on the inner, the equivalent of a chakra within your body, unfolding many petals of power, of Light and of Love. You are becoming, in fact, the body through which a spiritual Being may manifest, a group Being, a Being who will not manifest physically but will manifest through the channels provided by this center and many others throughout the world.

Therefore, see yourselves as building the body through which a cosmic Being will manifest, a Being unable to express on earth in any other fashion.

Those of you who travel away from this center are asked not so much to represent this center as to represent the cosmic levels inherent within your being, levels awakened and vitalized by the energies in this center. We also wish, and will manifest, the emergence of a clear and dynamic perception of the next phases of revelation beyond this period with the consciousness of men being involved in change.

You must become citizens, dwellers, within the New Age, fully attuned to limitlessness. We cannot tell you how to accomplish this; you will discover it for yourselves in your interactions, but in so doing you will release an explosion of Light within your beings and from there out into this center and the world beyond.

QUESTION: *Could you elaborate on the teaching aspect of Findhorn?*

All teaching is simply a means of providing a path for the being into direct contact with God. The teaching of Findhorn, to be perceived truly, must be seen in its totality and not as a specific part of that totality. That which is being taught here and revealed has less verbal form but is essentially a living force externalizing itself. It speaks and it acts. Even those who come from outside and contribute from their consciousnesses form part of the teaching of this center. Otherwise they would not be attracted here, nor permitted to speak. There are a multitude of patterns present in this center, only a few of which have been revealed. To see the teaching here, it must be considered as much as possible in the wholeness of the community and its activities. This is because we are seeking to attune you to very subtle realms beyond the physical, wherein lie your strengths and your attunements. Eventually Findhorn will evolve a teaching aspect in an outer sense.

This will be a center, a womb, in which many future teachers will be trained. Training is an insufficient term. They will be placed in contact with a supreme Form, sealed to that God within and then sent forth.

The key to Findhorn and all of its actions at this time is that it is a center for materialization; that is, blending the planes and making them one in expression, cooperation and harmony. This center is like a press, taking separate units and fusing them together and sending them forth as a wholeness and a unity: It is the job of this center to externalize, to provide, and increasingly provide a powerful force of manifestation, bringing down and calling forth from below and sealing the two together.

Just as my function has always been to release energy which flows throughout the vibrating body of earth, so is Findhorn a continuing aspect of that revelation, impregnating earth, humanity and the planes immediately beyond with energies to effect nuculear evolution.

QUESTION: *Could you enlarge on the term "nuclear evolution?"*

I exist within all things; my home is in the center of all. I am a point around which all manifest, the seed from which all germinate. As I seek to manifest a further aspect of myself, I unfold from within and vibrate from without that energy which is the signature of my further unfoldment. Though I speak to you as consciousness, my energy goes directly to myself within the atomic heart of you. Each atomic center, each nucleus anditsinner splendor, is me. I am all this, and as I unfold, it unfolds. It unfolds in response to my call, for I am within and I am without. I am you and you are I. As I send forth the energies, you respond with all the parts of your body and all the matter of which you are made. Consciousness knows no limit; there is no barrier to it. Your consciousness does not stop with you. It extends into the depths of your being and into the heights of interstellar space. There is no limit; not one part of earth can evolve but that all parts evolve. I speak of nuclear evolution, for in this I refer to this indivisible unity of earth which is, in its entirety, undergoing evolution — not only man in his human form and kingdom but all kingdoms, all matter, all energy undergo this transformation. The term focusses your attention on the microcosmic base through which this Light flows, as well as the universal, macrocosmic sources from which it descends.

QUESTION: *It has been seemingly revealed through some of us that there are twelve fully Christed Beings in the world at this time. Can you say anything about this?*

There is no place where Light is not. There is no heart where Love is not. The Christ is in all things and in all men. There are those who act as magnetic centers for revelation, but in the case to which you refer, it is largely the gathering up of the energies of the past and the receiving of them into the energies of the future. There are twelve and there are twelve and twelve to follow. There have been twelve; now arise twelve more who embody, purely, energies of the transmuted past and the revealing future. I have not sent all my messengers to you; only those who would be useful in clearing the way for those who would come after, who are now arising.

But I am where man chooses to look and see me. Even if he chooses to look within himself, there I am.

QUESTION: *You have spoken just now of Your messengers and earlier on you said that by coming together in this group, we form a new body through which a Being unable to express through any other fashion can express. Would you clarify this some more?*

There are Beings of Light and power who cannot take on human form, for they are far too extended in the range of their consciousness to be placed into any single kingdom. Their energies, their being, can express only through a vehicle composed of the united effort and blending of several kingdoms and people. Call them, if you will, Lords of the Sacred Centers or Lords of the Rays; they are limitless. Their bodies are the combined energy fields of countless people blended in love with beings of other evolutions. They are not group souls but they must function through a cooperative blending, for no one Being has the power, while in form, to manifest these cosmic entities. I cannot reveal myself through a single form; I reveal myself now through groups. As these groups expand and embrace the world, I shall be fully revealed, for I am all.

I am the Light within all humanity. I am the Love that has never passed from this world but has walked with Man through darkness. I am Man revealed, his hopes unfolded, for I am limitless, as is Man and all life. Receive my blessing into me, for we are one, and let it pour into our Body of the earth. I bless you all.

Chapter 5

The Revelation of Limitless Love and Truth

August 15th 1970

My beloveds, I wish to reveal to you my presence and to fill your consciousness with a vision that is of me, that through that vision your lives may be uplifted and welded together. So be it.

What is Limitless Love? Surely it is that presence which has been before the foundations of the earth and shall remain after this planet has entered yet another cycle in the far distant future of your time. I am timeless and infinite. There is no place that knows me not. There is no time when I have not expressed what I am. I am the root of you, I am the stem of you, the flowering and the seed that goes forth. I am all that you are. You will receive my energy and it shall dwell within you and make you one.

With whose voice do I speak? I speak with my own, but whose voice is that? Am I God? Am I a Christ? Am I a Being come to you from the dwelling places of the Infinite? I am all these things, yet more. I am the very life of you and there is not one creature upon this planet but what expresses me and yearns for me more fully. I am Life but I am not a Being. I contain all Beings. I am the Life from which all form springs. I am the womb and all must enter through me. But I am not a Being. I have no form but dwell in all forms, and thus may I greet myself within each of you and you know my blessings eternally from the center of you.

Yet I speak in preparation for a Being whom you have invoked in your desire to embody and to pioneer a new dimension of consciousness for mankind, a Being who is the Regent for energies brought from beyond your system. I am greater than He, yet less than He. If this is strange, then ponder it not but simply allow what I am to emerge within you. I take no form but I am in all forms. This is both my glory and my limitation. All who enter this planet must do so through me and I prepare the way and give them form. You are my center who provides the form for one who is of me but who is a Being and who comes to join the community of this planet.

I wish to present to you, therefore, the revelation of your pattern and the revelation of man's destiny, for behold! I have placed my seal upon this planet. I have sounded the call and I have been evoked and even now I dance my dance and sing my song within the heart of all things. I have transformed the planet. The Light does shine in the darkness though the darkness comprehended it not. Even now you dwell in realms different from your homes of but a few years ago. You dwell in me as has never before been possible, for I have revealed myself. All of life knows me in its deepest levels. I place this before you that my planet shall not be destroyed and shall in no way suffer, for that which I am cannot be destroyed nor can it suffer.

I am the Life which, having revealed itself, unfolds in growth and you are a manifestation of my growing as I emerge from within you and from within this community. You will hear rumours of destruction, of disaster and of the cleansings that man has invoked, but I tell you that all who are of me have passed that veil and dwell now in another realm entirely. You share this planet with others, others who hold me within them but know me not. What they invoke is not of your concern for they may see me in the thunders and lightnings and the tremblings of their souls as I burst my way free. Naught can contain me now unless it grows as I do. Heed not nor be concerned for the safety of the world, for I tell you now, it is contained within me.

Already I have handed over the world that was to those laws which shall shepherd it into its outworkings, and all who remain on the world that was, in consciousness and in life, are no longer subject to me save that I am eternally within them. They align themselves with other laws which are ordering change. But I and those who are invoked to this planet as

61

Beings of great Light and Love form the Body of a new heaven and we form the Body of a new earth. Man decides in which heaven he shall dwell in his consciousness and through that decision he decides which earth shall claim him and he shall be subject to the Laws of the earth that has claimed him. I proclaim to you, in spirit and in love, new laws, new life, new perfection, and daily I seek to grow within you. Open to me. I am within you. I am you.

Yet, though this revelation and change have occurred, there are links yet remaining between the two earths and the two heavens and many may yet cross. How shall I describe this except by saying that I consolidate myself, that there are many who are of me but know me not, yet in the days and weeks ahead shall hear my call and be drawn to me. The new heaven and the new earth are forming in your midst and this is the importance of this centre, that it is a magnetic point around which new spheres of consciousness may form. This is why all that has been revealed to you as change is of vital importance, for you must consistently, though at times gradually, align yourselves with the new heaven and the new earth. Then you are under my full protection and my full blessing and shall be increasingly so. As you grow and expand your consciousness, consistently remove from yourselves all of the old. This may be gradual but it must be consistent, for in this way you will remain protected and under my blessing.

Great changes have occurred in kingdoms beyond yours and they also are moving into a new heaven and a new earth. If man does not commune with them, he will be left behind and communion will be impossible. All is moving. You are moving not only through space and time but within a dimensional shift; you are moving within Light, Love and Consciousness.

I have been revealed as Truth, as Limitless Love, as Life, and I move steadily towards the consummation of my revelation. For I attract to me now Lovers from beyond the stars to unite with me and pour their seed into earth and transform it, Regents of vast new powers and energies to descend through many centers upon the earth.

So receive into your hearts my blessings and the knowledge of my presence and the knowledge that you move increasingly into limitless love and life. Align your hearts and thoughts with this and seek to represent what I am and what you are.

QUESTION: *You say that we are not to be concerned with the safety of the world, for it is contained with you, within Limitless Love, and that you have fully revealed yourself. Could you say a little about what did, in fact, happen in this period between 1961 and 1967 and whether 1967 was a culmination of your Revelation?*

I have done that which I manifested myself to do. I am now the Life of a new heaven and a new earth. Others must draw upon me and unite with me to build its forms. As I have said, be not concerned for the safety of the world. You are the world. Be not concerned for your own safety. That which happens to those who have come under different laws and a different cycle, I cannot influence. They have passed beyond me in my new revelation, though not beyond me as I slumber within them. They shall find me yet, though their way be long and the finding in the future. What they have invoked shall come to them, but it will manifest as beauty and as revelation and as release.

I work through life and through consciousness. Man must believe in me and be aware. Through him I may be revealed, as he is the builder of a new heaven and a new earth. I place myself before his awareness and continue to do this; through this yearning and expectation I have revealed myself. I have exposed myself through a new manifestation of my energies, and I now radiate through my Link, a single Source, not scattered, a single Source drawing to me the elements that will form the new heaven and the new earth and this motion proceeds irrevocably, inexorably towards its perfect revelation. My power has been liberated and all now move swiftly toward their appointed destinies as their consciousnesses have chosen. Your world shall become — and swiftly it shall become — two worlds. You will call one light and one dark,

63

but I am in both of them. Be not concerned about my ministry for those whom my new revelation cannot touch. Be only concerned with what I am in the new and in the now. You world cannot be touched. Their world is under their law and shall disapper.

I am acting within the entire vibrational structure of this planet on all of its levels. I unfold from within it what it has always stored there and which shall form the new. I invoke and invite from beyond Beings who come to impregnate me with powers and energies from what I am beyond this system. I obey the laws of form, though I am formless. I move through my beloveds on many levels though I am the Beloved of all and am on all levels. Not one of you, not one atom of life, stands beyond me. Shall I forsake those who even now drift apart into a destiny of their own, in a world of their further fulfilment? I am their shepherd as well and not one sheep shall stray except I go after it. But I must see my other sheep home, for it is their destiny and I cannot wait. So I am with you and I am with them. Not one man, not one creature goes apart from me. Be not concerned and sorrowful. Whatever befalls the old world, I am there and I am Life and I am Beauty and I am Joy and I am Perfection. Heed not the voices that speak to the old but know that I am within you, for I would proclaim to you what comes from beyond. I would have you unite with it and be impregnated with it as I am within you and receive from my greater Being beyond this planet.

Let these words go forth: I am with all men. I have been with them since the beginning of time. I shall walk with them forever. Their destiny is mine. Their life is mine. Their yearnings are for me and I seek to answer them. I await in the pavilion of my love for my lovers to come unto me that we may be united. Some will come straight away and the marriage feast be celebrated now; others have long journeys yet to take which they have set themselves; for they have heard rumours of far treasures that are not of me. But when they find them not, they will find the pavilion of my love and I shall join them.

If you speak with my voice and release my words, let it be as I would do, with hope, with joy, with promise, with love. I stand revealed and call all men unto me. All men may come. Let no man who hears my words feel himself lost, for he is only lost who heeds me not and seeks another lover. But he will find me too, one day. Be not concerned. All is well.

Let men not speculate to which world they belong. Their lives decide this. Their actions decide this. What are they creating as they move amongst me, as I am within all things, within humans, within nature, within all that is? How do they unite with me? That will decide to what world they belong. Increasingly, the worlds will move apart in consciousness until they are absolutely separate and perceive each other no more. For it is written that two will be at work in the vineyards; one shall be taken and the other remain. I shall snatch you up to me. This I have promised and this I am doing. You are with me now if you can but accept it.

Let my words go forth to be a signal to all my people that I am revealed and stand within them and all about them.

I speak within each of you always. You are my beloveds. Naught can separate us. Even if you turn me out, I am still with you. Even if you invite me not to your home, yet I am there. Even if you hear me not, I shall always whisper to you. You cannot lose me. You cannot hurt me. You are my beloveds and I am with you always. In the end of an age, in the beginning of an age and beyond, beyond time, beyond form, we are One. So it is, so it has been, so it shall always be. I bless you each with the fulness of my Being and I greet myself within you and I know that we are One. So be it.

Chapter 6

Obedience to Law

August 5th 1970

Unfolding across the pattern of earth are Light and Love blended and revealing themselves through my Body. Where gateways are created, I may enter and where I enter, I prepare the way for One greater than myself who comes to add new energies to earth. When last I spoke to you, it was with the intent of communicating the idea of this great Being whose form was being built upon this center and who would use the energies built up through the thinking and acting and aspirations of these people as the vessel through which He can manifest Himself to the world, just as He will manifest Himself in other lands and other centers in times to come. But there must be an entry point and this center has been selected to pioneer this entry point. He bears with Him energies new on earth and stimulating new responses from the earth and all its kingdoms. As it is written, you truly cannot pour new wine into old vessels; hence this great Light and limitless Love cannot enter nor manifest through the forms of man's actions and attitudes of the past.

You have long been told of a time of breakthrough and great expansion for this center. I tell you that time is with you now. This is a promise, but it is not a gift. Nothing that you have here is a gift save that you have so ordered your lives as to be open to the giving, and then abundance is poured out freely. But God will not transgress His Laws and with the incoming of new energies from Him and through the Regent of these energies, whose name is not to be given but who is Himself Limitless Love and Light and more beyond, new laws require manifestation. Hence we have presented to you together and singly glimpses of the necessity for changes in patterns at this time.

Not drastic changes but, as you will see, the perfect

66

outgrowth of all you have done to this point, and what you have done to this point has perfectly prepared the way in your training, each of you, and in your working and co-operation together. I would have you know there are present with you Beings of all the kingdoms concerned, for all are contained in me. We work to release these new energies into men.

I wish to discourse with you on the subject of law and obedience to it. Law is simply the form through which Life manifests itself for the benefit of itself. It is the presence of God's stability and order, without which there would be chaos.

But God's laws are not static. They are living realities of His Being and they expand as spirit expands and grows in form and matter. Jesus fulfilled the laws of his day and yet presented a greater law, that of limitless Love, that a man who lived in love would obey all the laws given in the past, for he would move in absolute consideration and sensitive awareness of the needs of his fellow men, which is what organization amounts to.

The Being who enters now as, shall I term Him, the Regent of New Age energies, can only manifest Himself through organization and order and obedience to law. Where law is broken, He will retreat, for if His energies are exposed to disobedience of law, His energies are distorted. This will not happen.

You are shifting, you are moving now into being a New Age center, not only a pioneering center with one foot in the old age and one foot in the new, but totally in the new. You must understand what this means and the changes it requires in your consciousness, your attitudes and your expressions toward each other. I wish to clarify this for you that there may be no misunderstanding. Men have created laws on many levels. Some of these laws seem unimportant and not useful; many of the children seek to break the laws which they do not like because they interfere with their freedom of expression. The New Age is freedom, but the New Age energies cannot abide where law is broken. Only the energies of the interim destructive period — if I may use that term and ask you to realize it in its positive sense of clearing away the old — only those energies can abide, but they are not of me and they are not of this great One whom I am assisting in His descent to earth. Therefore, all who would be of the New Age cannot break laws.

They must seek through the power of love to transcend the limitations of man's law. This can be done and will be done, because it must be done, or else you will remain an interim activity. Wherever you are, here or out in the world of struggling humanity, you are representatives of the New Age, which is love, sensitivity to others, consideration of their patterns, awareness of their needs and upliftment of all fulfilment through the affirmation of my presence. The mind may see that it must break a certain law to gain desired ends, but I tell you, now you cannot do this and remain in the presence of these New Age energies.

Great and powerful and loving forces have been invoked and anchored, but you must understand that these forces do not in any way place you, any of you, in a superior position to the rest of this my earth, but it makes you the servants of all through love, through light, through wisdom. If it means greater discipline upon yourselves, then this must be so. For now I would extend myself and this great One from cosmic reaches would extend Himself through you to struggling humanity. This cannot be done if humanity sees in any of you any action contrary to organization, to safety, to the ordered patterns that man has created. Man has many laws that are useless to God, but man must be inspired through the presence of Love to change them himself. You must work through that affirmation. There are others who will break the laws and may do so with impunity, even as it was possible to do so within this group pattern in times past. But now you have received an outpouring of special sanctification and it has increased your responsibility and your joy a thousandfold. You are examples of the new and people will find their eyes opened to you. People throughout the world will be attracted to you. What you represent to them must be absolutely in harmony with the patterns of Love, of Light and of awareness of the whole and the well-being of the whole.

In all of your activities your consciousness must expand into awareness of the whole through love, not only of humanity but of all the kingdoms who share this planet.

From my vision nothing will stop this, my center, from unfolding in perfect beauty, in glory impossible to describe. All kingdoms await to co-operate with you and become one with you, but they watch you now to see how the energies are used. Be aware even of small things where I am, in relationships with people, in simple things, in words that are spoken, in that which is pleasing to the eye and to the ear and to all the sense of man through which he apprehends the presence of others. Be perfect in all respects, not only in some. Each of you has been blessed and each of you in his own fashion receives the outpouring of this revelation to live within you. Respect it and nourish it as you would a tender blossom and allow it to unfold within you. It is a serious responsibility and yet a joyous one, for you do not carry it alone but in company with each other, in the support of the community, in the support of all life that attunes to you. It is important to realize this: you have become the bearers of new and potent energies and the patterns of past action, attitude and behaviour are no longer applicable. Therefore be aware in the moment; live in the now and know what you are doing, each of you, and see if it corresponds to the motion of this love and life and peace and trust in God.

I am Limitless Love. I embrace all that lives. I assist the descent of One from beyond this planet who carries New Age energies. We seek to break down the barriers between all men and all kingdoms of life, for our name is Oneness, Communion. This has been presented from several sources this week because it is of vital importance. The old ideas must go. The concept of love and communion, oneness and respect for all life in its own particular uniqueness, and blending with all life to create new patterns yet undreamed of — these are the concepts which I offer to you for the glorification of all life and the glorification of God.

QUESTION: *Could You enlarge please on the law of communion?*

Through the centuries man has looked upon himself as a separate species of life — one given dominion upon earth, as it is written and has indeed occurred. But imagine, if you will a king who by right of birth is given the throne and sits upon his throne and rules his people and all his land. He says to himself: "I am King. None may question me. All that I proclaim is right, for after all, am I not King?" Indeed he is king, but he will find that being a single source of God-life isolated within the concept of his kingship, his edicts will not flow in harmony with the needs of all life and lack of balance will result.

Communion means simply listening and becoming one with all the patterns that impinge on a given area of experience or life; to realize that man's greater glory and authority lie not in his standing alone upon his kingly throne but in stepping out of his palace and mingling with the populace. Jesus walked with the common man and became the greatest king the world has known, through the power of His Love. All things were brought within the scope of His Love, which knew no limit. This, then, is communion, that all that God has placed upon this earth aspires to perfection and expresses perfection in its own fashion; now each must seek to understand the other and to co-operate.

Man's consciousness has lost sight of this in the world. He does not know how to commune with his brother, nor with nature, nor with the vast spaces beyond; he cannot communicate with them. He is, as it were, a king who has been blinded, struck dumb, denuded of hands and feet and left powerless, save for the power of destruction. From my Being — as I manifest through this my center and others like it, though of different function, and as the great spirit of the New Age enters and externalizes itself through human awareness — man will learn to act in harmony with the whole, as a Regent of the whole, of man's interests and the interests of nature, of the interests of God, space and earth and all patterns that are brought within his ken. The powers that we place before you may literally transform the earth. Understand that these powers have not been released to men because man has not shown himself wise in his use of power, but you within this center have demonstrated a willingness to learn right use. You have demonstrated a dedication and a love that has opened to you this privilege and outpouring. But all kingdoms have an interest in this. What man terms perfection from his point of view is too narrow a concept and must be expanded to blend with the ideas of perfection from all of life's point of view. The earth is a single living entity; it is my Body. Please understand what this means. Understand what oneness implies and what it means to be the brain of the planet, which is what man is: the creative and directive source.

The patterns of New Age energy may only express themselves through obedience to law, which is simply stating that they must manifest through an organized channel. They are too powerful to be exposed to chaos. But law to us does not mean the same as rigidity or the crystallized forms that man has created. Within this center, an outpost of the New Age, new laws are being formed, laws born of Love and of Light and of the union of the two. But when you go out from this center, then you must flow with the laws of men, not obediently as one who says these laws are correct — for many of them are not — but as one who embraces the form within himself so that his love and light may transmute it.

Jesus as an archetypal example did not break law but He acted according to the dictates of love, and love cannot harm any man. But the first principle of love is a recognition of the needs and rights of others. All man's laws attempt to express this; hence they must be respected within their own patterns before they can be transmuted into higher ones.

In this center you will establish your own laws and this is proper, as you are guided by God and the inspiration of these new energies. But there are many souls now who are leading the elements of change as an interim energy who publicly, outwardly, break the laws of man's society. Many of these people are properly guided in so doing. But this my center, with its new attunements, must build new laws, not in opposition to those of men but in glorification of what man has always sought to do, giving to him a more perfect example.

Love simply never places itself superior to any man or any condition. It doesn't have to, for it knows that it can work within any condition and transmute it utterly and create perfect results. It is simply that you are evolving another role, that of exemplifying the presence of New Age laws.

Chapter 7

World Events

August 18th 1970

QUESTION: *In November 1961 you stated that world conditions would show evidence of the leading up to the introduction of a nuclear device that would bring about what you termed the final human level episode. You also spoke of a most sudden conflict breaking out between nations as the result of a war starting in Asia and spreading to the western world, and you stated that a human press-button device would be used and that simultaneously with the pressing of the button, instead of disaster, the universal Revelation would occur. We would appreciate as great a clarification as possible regarding the meaning and implications of this statement.*

My Beloveds, what is the revelation which I bring? It is that of universal life, life without ending, life that is all-embracing, life that cannot be destroyed, life that cannot be ended. It is life that is not contained simply in human level consciousness and form nor in the material world which surrounds you. It is life which manifests throughout all that I am.

You have witnessed only the play of form upon form and of the destruction of form by other forms of material nature. Now you have introduced into your world energies beyond form, at the heart of form, nuclear energies and for the first time, you can release energies to play directly upon form, subtle energies. I have proclaimed and revealed myself within these energies. They are of me. I form the substance of your world; I cannot be turned against myself. If these energies are released, they must express according to what I am, and I am Love. I am Truth. I am Light. I am beauty. I am joy, but I am life and more life in increasing abundance.

I have spoken to you of two worlds. I am the body of one; I am the shepherd of the other. The one is what I am and I

73

am revealed within it. The other knows me only as its shepherd, separate and apart. I do not live within it. I only stand and envelop it. It is under the control of other, older laws. The release of nuclear energies within these older laws will have a different effect from its release within me.

Men seek for peace because they are afraid. It is not peace which they desire. It is security and the safety to continue their explorations and manifestations of power. This safety and security is denied them. Those who reach for power shall receive it, but it will destroy them. No peace will be found on a human level of consciousness, and the drama of human level consciousness is soon to come to an end.

But there are other dramas continuing. Man may unite with me within himself and there he may find peace, but a peace that knows not fear, that is not personally afraid but can move into the world as a manifestor of what I am, Limitless Love and Truth.

Man is involved with a revelation beyond his power to cope with or encompass by himself on his human level of consciousness. A new level, a new humanity seeks birth; the new heaven and the new earth of which I spoke. This new humanity filled with my presence, cannot be touched by whatever falls upon the old. Should nuclear devices be used, the energies will be the revelation of me. All that will remain is of what I am and all that is not of me shall disappear, to follow another law and another destiny.

No man knows the time of my coming. I am already revealed all about you, if you will look within and about yourselves and see me. See naught but me, and know my presence with you. There is no waiting, but for those who choose to wait for the hour of my universal revelation, they will not know when it will occur. Behold! In the next second, I am.

All that is of the new seeks its birth and motion with me. It cannot be thwarted. I have nothing to do with the old in my new revelation. It is not of me in my new revelation. It is as apart from me as I have been from you. You see me not, yet you know my presence as the life within you and in this you are blessed. I remain with the old, but as a shepherd — but that is not of your concern nor is it the concern of what I am in my new revelation.

Man will not find peace in human level explorations, for he has no conception of what peace requires nor of what it demands of him. Peace is deeper than a simple cessation of conflict; peace is not the opposite of war. Peace is life and life abundantly overflowing its limitations. Peace is vital. Peace is growth. Peace is what I am. Seek me and you have found peace.

I would say that all I have stated is truth and shall manifest itself. Let no man who would be of me have fear. I have not come to sift the good from the bad. I am not the judge. I simply am what I AM. If you are that I AM, then you are of me. If you are not, then you come under a different law and must obey it before its cup can pass from your lips. I am Limitless Love guided by Truth. I am all things. I am all that harkens to my voice now; I am all that will hear my voice in the future, though that future is yet unborn.

Man must emerge from human level consciousness. This he will do, either through me or through his own invocation of old laws and all that that entails. Harken now to my words, for they are of extreme importance. Form no barriers between your consciousness and those of the world. I do not send you forth, who hear my voice, to proclaim the kingdom of the saved and the disaster of the lost. I have stated repeatedly, I am with all. None are saved. None are lost. There is always only what I am, but I have revealed myself in new life and new Light and new truth. Those who attune to that will not be saved. They will only be attuned to what I am in my new revelation. And those who heed me not, but follow the downward course as human level consciousness unwinds itself and enters a new cycle, they are not lost. They only attune themselves to what I will become in a future revelation to them, but apart and separate from what I am now.

If you would build the new as I call upon you to do, then

you cannot set yourselves against the old. There can be no separation. Your consciousness must perceive only the new and build towards it. I will state this: it is not **my** function through this center to proclaim **my** voice, though this has been done and may continue in the future. It is **my** function through this **center** to demonstrate what **I am** through the medium of group evolution. You are not a verbal revelation of **me**, except in a minor sense. You are a living revelation of what **I am** in the hearts and activities of man, nature and all life. **my** words are simply **my** medium to link you with me.

I have answered this question at length, for I wish you to understand that the law will be obeyed. The old will disappear. Human level consciousness by itself can no longer resolve the complexities it has created. It is enmeshed in conflict. Only conflict can be born, but out of this conflict will come **my** revelation. It is coming and it is here. I am now what I am and have always been.

The conflict in Asia has developed. It is spreading. It will engulf the consciousness of men. Indeed, it has already done so. Men everywhere live in universal conflict and fear. This will invoke its own laws and its own result. Turn, then, to my presence, but not as an escape. I offer no man refuge. Turn to me as the creation of the new. Be what I am, and you will only receive universal revelation.

When the energies of atomic power are released, they will be of Me and revelation will occur. But heed this: I am not prophesying war. **I am** the revealed future and in me there is no conflict. Let no man think I have placed upon him through Truth the inevitability of destruction, disaster and death. These are all illusions save to those who are not of **me**. What the old invokes that it may disappear need not disturb the new.

It is important for centers of this nature to build. I must be revealed. It matters not the form. All that you have built here may change in the twinkling of an eye, but if it does, it will change into what I am, into what you are building towards. Form is not important, only that you manifest what I am at all times. You are not building towards me. You are expressing what I am and it gives the illusion of growth and building. This is important and why I have stated that all that is of this center must be of the new, must be constructive, must build, must express what I am now.

What I am is not a form. I am Life and the spirit of Life. My new heaven emerges throughout the world, not only in this center or others like it, not only amongst those who have heard of me in this identity or have heard of me through the revelations of groups and minds attuned to the Light and to Limitless Love and Truth. I am growing within many who know me only in the context of the old and yet have truly grasped me.

Tell the young that the choice is not between forms but between consciousnesses. What I am cannot be resisted. If I live within them, I will direct them. I can work in an office, in a factory, in a school, in a temple, in a church, in a mine; I can work anywhere and be anywhere, for I am in all places. If they attune to what I am, they will find that I propel them perpectly beyond all forms that would encase them and leave them in the old.

Some may wish to come and should come to centers such as this. All who are of me will eventually commit themselves to the building of the new, no longer in conflict with the old, no longer in revolution. They will allow the dead to bury their dead and the old to pass away. This cannot be a mental process. Who is to decide mentally what is of me and what is not? First I must live within you. You must express what I am without limit and then all is revealed perfectly.

I want no man mentally to judge, for I have stated, I am not a judge. I simply AM and all who are of me will come and express what I am within them. They cannot resist it. No matter where they are, they will transform their surroundings or they will leave their surroundings. They will have no choice, nor would they wish a choice. Therefore, tell the young and all whom you meet that there is a choice between heavens. Do they wish the paradise of the old with its particular lures, or shall they become one in consciousness with the heaven of what I am within them and in this living world, in loving care for all its life, in communion with all its beings? The heaven that they choose to dwell within and to aspire towards in their consciousness will determine the earth on which they reside and which shall claim them with its laws. For the young in school, they are not bound by the forms of their school if they can become one with me and allow that living intuition and life and truth to reveal their destiny and their path.

I wish you to go beyond the mind. I speak not to the mind. I speak to what I am. I am greater than words. To find me, go beyond what I say and be what I am. Each man will make his own decision. You need advise him only of my presence, of my Life, of my limitless outpourings of joy and abundance to him, if he will but accept it and live according to my law, which is the character of what I am within him.

I will say this, as well: though no man knows the time of my coming, though it may be in the next second and though it will manifest universal revelation and change, if you would be of me, understand that I have revealed myself. Do not wait. Do not hold any activity in abeyance, feeling that I may yet come. I have come and am coming. Meditate on this and you will know what I mean. One is for what I am in the new, the other for what I am amongst the old. You must — all men who hear my voice must, if they would align with me — not wait but act, knowing that I AM revealed and they may begin to build the new heaven and the new earth. Remember that you are building more than forms; you are expressing what I am. This is all I ask. It is what is most important.

I am a constant presence in this center, amongst its people, flowing from the kingdoms of nature and from all that this center represents. I am revealed throughout the world and I am a constant presence throughout the world as I form and am now the new heaven and the new earth. I speak of consciousness and life, which form must obey and will obey. Hear me within you. Live my life. Be what I am. So be it.

Chapter 8

The Age of Man's Maturity

September 2nd 1970

I greet myself within your consciousnesses not as new
revelation but as that which is revealed and as that which
clarifies its presence. That which has occurred and is
occurring is not strange, for it follows the very pattern of life
instilled in this planet when it was conceived by God. I have
walked with you since that time. That which is different now is
that I would walk with you in even closer measure and greater
sharing. You have been carried like an infant in the arms of
Love and Truth. When you became stronger you were placed
upon your feet and allowed to run about as a child. Then you
became a youth of consciousness and sought your independence from me and all that I represent. I stand revealed to
human consciousness as that gift of independence for man.
You have sought it, you have desired it, you have longed to be
a god as is your destiny. Can you now accept the maturity of
your being and all that it requires of you? Can you enter the
world as a mature being, no longer a youth in consciousness?

This I place before man: that he must cease his
rebelliousness, for it ill becomes one who is upon the threshold
of maturity to behave as one still in the thraldom of
adolescency. Man has desired his independence, he has sought
the flaming crown of free will. Receive then what you have
invoked. No force can halt man's reception of what he invokes,
for all that is of God and all that is of me obeys the law. You
are placed out of the nest, for you have drawn this moment to
you. Can you withstand it?

I say that I am your strength and I am the revelation of
your maturity. Do not think that this new heaven and new
earth which emerges from the womb of the old is in any way a
judgement; it is the arrival of that which Man has himself
invoked, the moment when he is thrust out of his sheltered

79

world into the real world, the world of cosmic law and cosmic consciousness, where he must begin to take up the responsibilities of a householder of the Divine, where he must begin to marry the Divine Beloved and set forth on his heritage of new creation. You have drawn this to yourselves. Think not that your prayers and invocations to God through centuries of time go unheeded and when your responsibilities and maturity arrive do not seek to thrust them aside. You cannot escape what you have invoked and any who would thrust it aside and seize not the sceptre of responsibility and the crown of illumination thereby pledges himself to continued adolescency.

This is the separation of the two worlds. First in consciousness, secondly in energy, ultimately in form, it is the separation between those who cleave unto God, their Beloved, in new revelation and new maturity and those who remain in the household of their Father, yet do so in rebellion as, in spiritual adolescency, they seek their own Divine Identity. For those who remain in adolescency of spirit, the law will treat them accordingly; those who grasp what I am as the Beloved in new revelation of what man is capable of will come under a different law and a greater freedom.

Listen then to what I say, for I speak not of myself apart from you but of what I am within you. I have stated that I am Love and as Love I embrace all things. I am in conflict with none; I am the servant of all. Be thou likewise in your maturity of what I am. I am Truth; it is truth that separates the worlds. It is truth that separates those who can receive the heritage of manhood and those who cannot but who must remain within the allowance of adolescency. Creative man, mature man blending in love and truth with his environment to build the new heaven and the new earth receives his just wages which are limitless in their abundance of life, of joy and of the unfoldment of all God's blessings. Those who cannot accept their maturity and the responsibilities which it demands can only receive that allowance given to them that they may survive, that they may grow, until one day they too will enter the real world and leave their illusions behind.

Those who come and dwell in centers such as this which have as their function the building of a pure New Age civilization and the externalization of what I am in new revelation can have nothing to do with the old. This is the working of truth. As you look out upon your world you must see it in its perfect state, for that is the reality that exists now that I am revealed. You are in a centre such as this not to heal the old but to build the new. Let your energies be thusly consecrated.

As you become as one with what I am as new spiritual life and maturity within you, you will form new links with what I am in the old world of adolescency. These links are important and represent the channels through which the revelation of your life in a center such as this may flow out to stimulate and encourage the new wherever it seeks to emerge. For those who hear my words and dwell not in a centre but dwell amongst yearning mankind, my words are different, but the message is the same. They, too, must see the new without any questions, without any doubts. See mature man emerging; reach through Love to touch the consciousness of those who surround you, not so much through words, but through the living demonstration in your affairs of what I am, as Love and as Truth.

Understand this wherever you are; I speak not to the mind. I do not ask any man to separate himself in conflict with the old, for this cannot be done if you would be of me. When you become mature you put away the things of your childhood, but you carry with you all that that childhood may offer of strength, of joy, of beauty and of wisdom. Heed not the forms of the old but be at one with all who dwell upon this earth. Two worlds there are and two worlds there shall become in consciousness, in life, in activity. But you are not the cutting edge of the sword which shall divide mankind. I ask you to be filters, gateways to the new, and to see all men as your brothers and as what I am within them. Act with love as I

81

am Love and see all men in the newness of their being. Should any not respond, release them in your consciousness and know that I am with them.

That which occurs now upon the earth is the reception of a new maturity of consciousness. If you would receive it you must change and become mature, adults under spiritual law who live and demonstrate the reality of what I am within themselves. An adult does not become distressed when a child cannot do the same as he. He releases the child to its own level of learning. Do you likewise with the world. I have stated that I am the revealed future and in me there is no destruction. There is no suffering, but there is change and there is a new maturity for those who can accept it and a continued adolescency for those who cannot.

Ponder not the mechanism of my change; build the new, build what you are, discover what I am within you and allow my Force, my Love, my Truth to handle all else. Unite with me and all is made plain. I am not a judge and all who would be of me cannot judge who comes and who stays and how the division will manifest itself. Live the revealed life and all else accomplishes itself perfectly.

That which I represent and that which I call forth from within you is timeless. Your maturity has been with you since the beginning of your creation. You cannot lose it; you will all gain it one day and that day, for those who can accept, is here now. Through a transformed humanity, creating a new heaven and a new earth, and through the force, maturity and openness of their consciousness allowing the presence of this new heaven and new earth to manifest itself, the earth that you have known will change and transfigure itself into matching beauty. Therefore let my revelation be one of hope, one of joy, one of love and one of truth. I separate no man. I simply stand and I call all men unto me. Come if you will; if you come, unite with me, your Beloved, and in your new maturity of being create with me the new heaven and the new earth to be our dwelling place together.

Be at peace, all of you. No man walks alone. I repeat this

again and again. I have stated that you must separate yourself from the old so that you can build the new, but in doing this you do not separate yourself from what I am within the world and within mankind. As you build what I am in the new world by revealing me in your lives, you transform all that is. Do this for my sake and for yours. Your world is already very, very separated, far more separated than I would achieve. Though my revelation brings separation in consciousness, I am not a divider; I am that which unifies. See me this way. Let what I am as Love and Truth live within you, and you will unify the world in its new aspects. Be what I am and all is made plain.

I extend to all of you Peace, Love, Truth and that blessing that comes to a being when it stands on the threshold of its manhood. All beings upon the earth may now enter into that maturity which they have invoked and which is rightfully theirs. Go ye forth then, with that blessing. Be fruitful in your consciousness united with me and together we will build and replenish the earth and multiply the blessing of the new heaven. So be it.

Chapter 9

Clarification of the Relationship between the Old and the New

September 3rd 1970

I am Limitless Love and Truth. I am the body of a new heaven and a new earth. If I am this body, then the new heaven and the new earth must manifest my characteristics, and anything which does not manifest my characteristics is not and shall not be of the new.

I have also stated that I am within all things and have been with the earth even before its foundation as a planetary body. I have expressed myself within the earth throughout its history. I am not a new revelation in the ultimate awareness of my presence. The reality of what I am has been with you always, but I am a new revelation and the time is here for man and for all kingdoms of Light to manifest an increasing display of my characteristics. Though I have been potential within the earth, I am now no longer a potential but a living reality which gives to Limitless Love and Truth greater power over the affairs of earth than before.

I have stated that there are two worlds, one of the old, one of the new. I have stated that I am in both of them. I have revealed myself through this revelation on many levels, not simply on the level of your sensory awareness. The potential of what I am has been made manifest and is a potential no longer, but a reality. This living reality is the substance of the new heaven and the new earth. These are only now being formed; the substance is only now clothing itself in physical forms, but the substance is there and is active and forms will develop accordingly.

Is there any place where I have not revealed myself? Indeed, there is: within the hearts and minds of all of those for whom Limitless Love and Truth is not a reality but still a potential. The old world is that realm of Consciousness and Being in which I am still only a potential not being expressed. This does not mean that I am not there. I am in all. It means that there I am only a potential, a promise, a hope.

Let us consider the planes of earth, one by one, that you may have a clear understanding of this. Through my revelation I now control and am ensouling all of the etheric plane of earth, that plane from which the earth derives its substance. This means that all upon the earth must derive its life and substance from me in my expanded revelation. I am now the body of the earth. I am that primal, basic energy level from which even the nucleus of your atomic structure on physical levels must draw its sustenance if it is not to collapse inward and become purely etheric. All physical manifestations of energy must now derive their being from me and I am in control of all of them. Anything which does not recognize me and will not provide, through the power of its life and its demonstration, channels for my energy to flow through, cannot derive energy from me. Any such being or thing therefore finds itself cut off from all source of sustenance, except that which is of its own Divine nature. This means that the old no longer has growing or magnetic power and must simply begin to disintegrate. From my standpoint it is already dead; it has changed its form and it no longer exists. I am all that exists and I reveal to man, that he may lift his consciousness and see the reality of this.

I am in control of all sources of energy from which you ultimately derive your physical existence. Any physical form that cannot draw upon me will simply run down. It will move into greater states of confusion, of chaos, of destruction in the sense of disintegration. The same process occurs when the integrative life-force of your being, your soul, departs from your physical self. The body then enters the process of decay and disintegration, which is not a negative action but part of the Divine process of circulation and the return to raw material.

On the level of nature, the nature kingdoms have responded to this change and are aligning themselves with it, so that they continue to receive life-force from the earth and remain part of the earth. This means that their energies of nourishment have altered and can flow only to those plant, animal and human forms which can accept such nourishment. Any form that cannot do so will find itself increasingly cut off from the nature forces and sources of natural energy and light and will simply disintegrate or be unable to reproduce itself. The presence of radioactivity upon your planet will render sterile all forms which cannot attune to new energies and will make them incapable of reproducing themselves. This is one action that is taking place, though I do not suggest that this is the totality of the change; it is only one phenomenon which is occurring.

The old will disappear fairly swiftly because the only power upon which it can draw is the power of its momentum, the power which it generates through its own patterns of habit and of inertia, which are fundamentally patterns of conflict. When I speak of the old, I do not necessarily refer to all that has gone before in the past. I am not referring primarily to an aspect of time, but I am referring to that which cannot manifest itself in my terms of Limitless Love and Truth, but maintains itself within the vibratory elements of conflict, chaos, negation and lack of responsibility. These energies of the old, of the limited and separative way of approaching life, are the only energies which the old can draw upon, which means that the old will draw upon sources of energy which are intrinsically destructive and disintegrating.

I have stated that the old is under laws other than what I am and must obey those laws. It will disappear. It may disappear quite swiftly, it may disappear more gradually. It matters not what happens to the old; from my point of view it no longer exists. That is the point of view which I seek to reveal to your consciousnesses. Men may now ask what the relationship between the two worlds is. I have stated that I am revealed and the separation has occurred. All that can exist upon the earth must now attune to what I am as the new etheric structure of this planet and the source of its life. This is irrevocable. This change in stabilization has occurred and the earth itself is now within a new age, which gives a sentence of absolute doom through change upon all that cannot attune to this. However, though I have revealed myself and stabilized myself, moving from a state of potential into a state of greater reality of expression, this does not in any way place a barrier on any man's consciousness. All who hear my voice in understanding of what I say and will make the necessary effort in their lives to manifest what I represent will move increasingly into the new heaven and the new earth.

I am Limitless Love and Truth. I am outside of fear; I am outside of hatred; I am outside of separation; I am outside of conflict and negation. A man who would be of me may not feel able to make a total leap, although he can if he so chooses. Let no man feel discouraged by his apparent unworthiness, for that is illusion. It is only required that you make consistent steps each day to change yourself. Even if they are small steps, they must be consistent and you must not be discouraged. Each day must show some increasing change into greater awareness of what I am and what the new earth and the new heaven require. If you are making these changes, then you are of me. Though you may not be able to love all men, if you can stop hating any man and begin to move only in tolerance and in a willingness to listen, you have placed yourself under my care. I will expand that small seed into a full tree, a full flowering of Limitless Love and Truth. There must be small steps if you cannot make large ones. This is all I ask.

You must stop indulging in those patterns of mind and emotion which represent the old. If you feel unworthy and unable to make this change in your lives, I say that this is illusion. Start in a simple way in a small area of living and I will pour forth my greater life within you to enlarge it. You must have trust and faith in yourself and in me and I will manifest and reveal myself to you. Know that you do grow, if you work consistently to do so.

No man is prevented from coming into the new heaven and the new earth, but there will come a time when the change is irrevocable, when the gap has become too wide and those who have not made that leap, that entrance, will find themselves moving off, out, within — who can say the direction — but out of the awareness of the new. They will remain in that area and state of consciousness suitable to them in their adolescency; but I will be with them and in future days I will reveal myself to them when they allow such revelation to occur.

Since what I am now is Limitless Love, no man who attunes to me can judge and feel himself superior to any other man. No man can speak of the kingdom of the saved and the kingdom of the lost. In my consciousness there is only Oneness and Love, but because I am also Truth, man must recognize the division that is taking place. This is the paradox of this time, and yet not a paradox. If you can love and still be at One with all, as I am at One with all, whether they move forward or stay behind, and still recognize that this change is occurring, then you have solved the paradox. Truth solves the dilemma of Love; Love solves the dilemma of Truth.

There will grow increasingly upon the earth centers such as this one; they should be isolated to some degree, for here you build the new world and must become purely the new world. Those who are part of such a center cannot look back upon the old. Does this mean that they are cut off from all who knew them in the past? It does not. It means that they are cut off from all those attitudes and actions that maintain the imbalance and limitation of the old.

I have not come to heal the old. The time for healing is past. I have come to build the new and I have come to shepherd the old into a place of its further outworking. I have stated that no sheep that is lost shall go unsought. I seek all my lost sheep; but first those sheep which have not strayed must be shepherded to their place of new destiny in order to arrive at their appointed hour. Hence this division occurs. As you build the new, the old is transformed. Understand this: you cannot heal other people now involved and engrossed in the limitations and the adhesive conditions of the old world and its thought-forms by attempting to pull them loose through brute force of mind or emotion. As you build the new, you add the power of living truth and demonstration to the thought-forms of the new. This power of proof, on a concrete level, will be the great revelation which will shatter the tyranny of the past and of the old.

This is why I have stated that all who would become part of a center such as this one cannot allow their consciousness to return to the old even through compassion, for the most compassionate action that they can make is to channel their energies into building, realizing and demonstrating what the new has to offer. Then they send out energies and ideas with tremendous magnetic qualities which will attract people and free them to a far greater extent than compassion would do. Understand that you look upon a world of form when you see suffering. Form has little meaning to me, for I am concerned with that which is the eternal life of you, the Divine Presence which I nourish and embrace. If forms must be destroyed that this Presence be released, then so be it. I am not ruthless, for I am Love; but I am Love and Truth combined and I move to bring about the total blessing of man, not momentary alleviation of some perpetual cycle of torment which will only repeat itself again and again. Strike to the root cause; change man's thinking and conceptual patterns and you will have done a greater service than simply by commiserating with the suffering of the world. This is my word for those who form New Age centers. Isolate yourselves somewhat. Receive what the Cosmic Ones would pour out to you; receive it through discipline, through harmony, through some form of order. Live the life of Love and Truth. Isolate yourselves from the thought and thinking of the world — which thinks in terms of healing that which is already dead and gone — and build the new.

You cannot heal a corpse, nor do we have any wish for you to do so. The old must pass away. It has served its purpose in the cycles of evolution and must now make way for a new, more expanded and more fruitful manifestation. Yet you can nonetheless see the perfect Presence of the Divine within the world and within the people who apparently dwell in the old. Through seeing this Presence, you call it forth. This is resurrection. This is the highest form of compassion and love. It links you with people, but not on the level of their pain and suffering, the level of the old which passes away. It links you with them on the level of the whole, of the new, of the perfect and of the resurrection. This calls the resurrection forth from the old world and raises the world and its people into the body of the new, which I am. This resurrection is happening now.

For those who are not part of centers such as this, the following is my word, as I would clarify your relationship with the old world: you cannot judge the world, only the state of your own consciousness. You must change your own individual consciousness and be what I am. Then your world will change. Though you may be an isolated person, alone in your belief and your change of consciousness, it matters not. If you are of me in your living action, then you are linked to all centers, to all others, to all that is of the new heaven and the new earth and their power is yours. Do not attempt to judge people. Do not attempt to save people. Demonstrate. Demonstrate. Live the life and release the energies accordingly. Be the New Age wherever you are. I am in all places. I am not restricted if you must seemingly work within the old world and its forms of activity. I am not concerned with the forms of the old. I am concerned with the consciousness of the new. Be prepared to voice revelation to those who ask to those who are open and when the time is appropriate to plant the seeds for a new harvesting of ideas. Do this not to force anyone to change, but as the demonstration of New Age joy and love and truth within you that changes you.

You are in the world to have contact with it, just as those who enter such centers as this one have a different function, which is to build purely the patterns of the new. Because you are in the world does not mean that you cannot be purely of the new. You must be of the new in your consciousness. By this

I mean that you no longer react to the world through attitudes of the past which are of fear, of hatred, of prejudice and of separation. You must be what I am. You must learn discrimination, which is Truth, and you must learn to manifest Love.

If, then, it is deemed wise for you no longer to remain in patterns of the old world earth, you will be withdrawn to other patterns, such as into a New Age center. Always be prepared for change. I have stated that all may change in the twinkling of an eye and you may find yourselves in another world of consciousness, opportunity and behaviour entirely. Man does not recognize what is occurring about him. He does not yet have the mental framework to comprehend it properly. So I do not attempt to speak to the mind, but to place before you the revelation that if you live the life suggested you will attune to me and I will reveal all that you have need of.

All of these changes man has invoked upon himself; I have stated that they represent the arrival of his time of maturity. This is what you have desired on all your levels and now it is here. The mature being is the one who is aware of the needs of the whole. Since he is part of the whole, he is aware of his own needs as well, but no longer as an isolated and selfish entity. He sees that by answering the needs of the whole, he answers his own needs, and that the reverse is also often true. He finds that balance between his need and the good of the whole. He is the entity who works in Love and in Truth. He walks and works in life as a partner with God, the Beloved. Anything less than this, or anything less than a sincere and consistent attempt to manifest this, is not maturity. A consciousness which is too tied to its own self is still adolescent and must invoke the laws of such isolation.

Therefore, I place before you the two worlds. Fundamentally they are worlds of consciousness, but in a very real sense they are literal worlds of form and energy. Wherever outlets are provided in your physical form world for the entry of the energies which are now the true etheric body of the earth, these energies will enter. You will find yourselves becoming outposts of the new earth with a true and very definite energy differential existing between you and your surrounding environment. These energies will in all ways seek to express through physical matter and ultimately will do so. If too great a stress of resistance is created to them, then the energies will work to shatter that resistance. If the resistance is in human consciousness, the new energies will remove that resistance within those human beings who have ceased to be nourished at the breast of the new earth and the new heaven.

I am revealed and in Me there is no destruction of any kind. For all who become part of me and are nourished by these new energies and new life — the new life verily of their own being — there can be no destruction. They will attract only creative energies into their lives. I am an outpouring of grace upon the earth. Any man who accepts this outpouring need not go through the trials and tribulations of the past. If he is willing to release and change himself and open to what I am and express it in his life, the past is finished for him; but he must, if he be relieved of the past, accept the responsibility of the present and be mature, even if that maturity requires him to make a great sacrifice of his attitudes and all that he has built up in a physical way throughout the past, even moving to a new place and into a new life. The changes will be different for each man.

I emerge, a new earth and a new heaven emerge, through the hearts and minds of those who can receive and express them. Those who cannot will remain part of the old. I place before you that there exist destructive forces which man himself has created. These forces do not have the power to affect any man who is of the new. Those who remain within the thought patterns of destruction and separation and who create these in their relationships with others will attract these forces to them, for these forces represent the heaven and the body of the old earth, although not entirely, for I am the Light and Life and Hope of the old, and I will go with it in my potential state. Yet I do stand before you now in my revealed state for all who can accept this revelation and move forward. I am open to all men, wherever they are.

This is the change and the choice presented before you. It cannot be decided through the mind nor through intellectual acceptance alone, but only through the acceptance of one's spiritual maturity, however small the degree a person can manifest. Once he has accepted that maturity, he must manifest it in increasingly greater degree and be what I am. All else is unimportant. How the worlds will separate is not of your concern. From my standpoint they are already separate and the old does not exist. You cannot be in conflict with the old, for you cannot be in conflict with what does not exist. If you are in conflict with anything through resistance, hatred or fear of it, you are automatically of the old to that degree. This is why I have stated that all who would be of me must build the new consistently and manifest the energies I represent. This is not being blind to the world. It is being open to the real world.

You who are outside of New Age centers will receive and will be strengthened by the power flowing from such centers. You will be able to demonstrate, in the manner in which you are guided in the moment, to be bridges for people who have yet to hear and have yet to know of this change. You will be my instruments for revelation, not necessarily primarily in your words, but through your lives. This is important. It is as important as are these centers, for there must be outlets for the power which is generated in them. You who seemingly live in the midst of the old world, even if you are completely isolated, are my outlets for the new heaven and the new earth. This does not place you in a superior position. It places you in a position of being the servant of all. This has always been true. This does not mean that you are to adopt a meek and humble manner, but to be proud and aware of the tremendous cosmic heritage that is yours in sharing with all men, and to realize that through that heritage and because of that heritage you can work to be of service to the All in all.

You must find the balances, learning through experience

how best to reveal what I am. That is the function of a group of this nature, to reveal these things consistently. I will not give you the answers; that is not my function. You must work it out for yourselves. Wherever you are, if you do not understand my words, go within and begin on as simple a level as you can comprehend. Live the life of Love and Truth and be at peace.

I am Oneness and all who are of me must realize this Oneness and see that there is no real separation. In revealing a New Age I do not divide brother from brother, father from son, mother from daughter in the ultimate sense of the Oneness which we all share, but in terms of physical personality relationships I can be a sword that divides and separates. You must be prepared to accept this and not resist it if such separation occurs. Release them to me, no matter where their destiny leads them. Also, you must not respond to the old with the personality. All responses must flow from the higher level of Love, of Light, of Truth, of Joy and of Wisdom. Whether the old is what you see on your television, whether it is within your family or within the suffering of mankind, you must see it impartially. You must see it in its perfect state. You must not allow your personality to interfere in fear, in anxiety, in pity. You must allow yourself to relax and see it in its new and perfect state and allow the Love and power of the higher nature to flow to it accordingly. Let your awareness flow out in this way as you build the new, and realize that by building the new you are giving power to those thought-forms of Peace, of Love and of Truth which must ultimately triumph upon the earth.

I spoke of the nature kingdoms which have changed in consciousness and energy, which is why man must learn to respect and to commune with them. Communication would be impossible if the nature kingdoms progress and man stands still. The nuclear level of life has also changed, as I have stated. I am now the energy active within that level in which is rooted all physical manifestation. From this point forward nothing can manifest on this planet save that it draws from me. Everything else is simply going under the momentum

94

built from the past, a momentum which is essentially destructive and which will run out. It is a clock winding down, as I have stated. This is why human level consciousness is coming to an end, for it does not have the power to maintain itself and to grow. Super-human level consciousness, that of man united with me, is only now beginning and I am the revelation of New Age Man.

All other levels of energy will follow suit. I am the new heaven in the emotional, mental and super-mental realms, now manifesting themselves with increased power. All thought, all feeling now have increased power, either to resolve themselves and disintegrate, or to build themselves through being attuned to the nourishing source which I am and through that attunement being able to receive New Age energies. These will augment beyond belief the power of thought and feeling to manifest, in your physical realm, things which exist on the Inner. You are coming to a time when, to an increasingly greater degree, you will be able to manifest and create through thought and through feeling. You already do this, but your power in this is being augmented. You have termed it instant manifestation; it will become far more instant than you believe is possible.

Let each man, therefore, make consistent steps, even if small ones, to manifest what I am, to grow and to expand in his Love, in his Light and in his Truth. This is all I ask. You do not have to leap directly to the mountain top. Those who can, should do so. Those who can only crawl to the foot-hill must crawl, but they must learn to crawl faster and then to walk and then to run. You must grow consistently. Each day allow your steps and your growth to be greater than the day before. In this way you manifest my unfolding revelation and you are of me. No man is unworthy of me if he will but accept and begin to change his life accordingly and to manifest what I am. In this way, my revelation shall grow, in centers such as this and amongst people throughout the world. The new heaven and the new earth shall emerge, not in conflict with the old but in revelation of its own being and its own values. The best way you can help those within the old is to build the new, for then you add power and light and energy to those patterns which represent now the salvation, nourishment and growth of this planet into its appointed destiny.

So hear my words and seek to demonstrate what I am. Then shall revelation truly live upon the earth and the new heaven and the new earth shall be manifested for the true healing, the true exaltation and the true fulfillment of all humanity and the launching of the new humanity into a cosmic brotherhood, a cosmic heritage and a destiny within the infinite.

I extend to you each my love and blessing. We are one. Live my life. Be what I am. I am Limitless Love and Truth.

Chapter 10

New Age Energies and New Age Laws: An Article

In all areas of human living and experience we are entering a New Age of consciousness and activity. One of the characteristics of this is the revelation, over the past few years, of new sources and kinds of energy and the utilization of these energies for human progress. An example of this on the physical level is the discovery of nuclear energy and the development of means of tapping this energy. With such discoveries comes the corresponding revelation of new laws for handling such energies with safety and economy. For example, the presence of radiation in the utilization of nuclear power makes it necessary to obey certain laws of safe use, such as proper shielding and decontamination procedures, if this source of energy is not to become a hazard instead of a help. Also with electricity one must obey laws of insulation and proper conduction so that people are not exposed to "live" currents which might electrocute them. Energy is neither positive nor negative; it is neither a help nor a hurt, but it can be either depending on how it is used, in accordance with the laws of right use or in ignorance or disregard of them.

Beyond the physical level, the New Age is also introducing into the realms of consciousness and spirit potent new energies, energies of transmutation, stimulation and materialization which have the capacity, as they move within and through the life and consciousness of man and his world, of building a new heaven and a new earth. Some of these new energies give far greater impact and power to an individual's thinking and feeling and liberate within him a fuller ability to create in his environment the externalization of his inner, subjective states of being. In the hands of a person or a group that was disorganized or negative in thought and feeling, these energies would intensify the projection of much chaos and negation into that individual's or group's environment. Obviously, this cannot be allowed.

Since many of these new energies create a potency within consciousness and the realms of thought and feeling every bit as powerful and in some cases more powerful than nuclear energy within the realm of matter, there is a necessity for these energies to be released to man and expressed by mankind under the control of certain laws. Such laws provide the structure or the order within which these energies can flow in safety. Indeed, until such a structure of understanding and obedience to these laws exists in human consciousness, these energies will not be released to mankind. They are too powerful to be exposed to chatotic, undisciplined and personality-oriented forces within the human mind and heart lest such chaos be strengthened and externalized to an intolerable degree.

Therefore, we are given certain laws of consciousness and action to be followed. Most of these are well-known. The greatest is the law of love. The presence of love within an individual is essential before he will be entrusted to receive true New Age energies. He must be able to think in terms of the whole as he plans his thoughts and actions. He must transcend a purely personal and selfish viewpoint and enter into a communion of love and giving and receiving with the whole of which he is a part. His love must be without limit. He must become harmless, unable to will harm to another being deliberately and out of a spirit of fear, hatred or competition. He must be limitless love. That is the first law and the most important one, for through love he expands his vision beyond his own seeming limitations and lives in awareness of the whole of which he is a part. Hence, he must love himself as well, not as a private, selfish entity but as a unique and meaningful expression and part of the whole.

Another important law is the expression of truth. Truth in this sense does not necessarily mean words that are true. It means the exercise of that faculty of discrimination which sees what is the right action at any given time. Truth does not accept all things to itself; it accepts only what is right and true for that time and place, but it does this without needing to judge on the ultimate rightness or wrongness of the person, thing or concept under its discrimination. Truth does not judge. It organizes by discrimination between what is useful now and what would be useful later and what has no more use at all. Truth and love must be expressed together. One balances the other. Love enables truth to grow and expand its discriminatory powers without allowing them to settle into a crystallized pattern of judgment and organization. Truth protects love and gives the power of appropriateness to the energy of love. To accept all things and all people is often the way of love; truth tempers this acceptance with a keen perception of what is right in the moment and prevents the energy of love from being dissipated over too wide a field or from being taken advantage of.

This brings us to a third law, that of responsibility to the cycle of energy flow. All energies that flow out from a centre must return to that center to complete the cycle. Also, energies received by a center must be balanced by a commensurate outflow from that center. Love gives all that it has to whomever has need. Truth demands that a return be made from those who have received, so that the law of completing the cycle is obeyed.

It has been possible in the past for individuals and groups to receive without giving back to the source in return. With New Age energies this is no longer possible. These powerful energies cannot enter where laws are not obeyed. Thus, an individual or group must respond in some fashion in order to return energy to the source from which it was received. If this doesn't happen, the pipeline is left open; everything is flowing in one direction only. Imbalance results and there is a waste of energies.

There is no room today for wasted energies. There is too much to be accomplished. These New Age energies will not carry a person along; he must work with them and give of his energy of life to increase the flow, to augment the power. In this way he can receive without limit. Man is weighed down with the inertia of centuries-old thought-forms which must be broken up and dissolved. Power must be concentrated in order to do this; the energies supplied from cosmic sources must be used rightly, appropriately, wisely, pinpointedly if they are to accomplish their desired ends. They cannot be wasted or exposed to chaos without being withdrawn. They must strike human consciousness with sufficient impact to effect a true and lasting inner change, to manifest a new and irresistable revelation.

Some pioneering individuals and groups, attuned to the universal unfoldment and well-being of humankind and of Nature as well, are receiving these pure New Age energies. In order to do so, they have had to undergo preparation and purification and they must now obey the laws under which these energies manifest themselves, laws ensuring the safety of human consciousness, ensuring that during this tremendous change into a New Age, chaos will not result. Such groups must function as manifestations of limitless love and truth, moving in awareness and sensitivity to the needs of the whole and moving with protection, discrimination and sufficient organization to ensure that these energies are not wasted but are given the direction and motion which will have the greatest impact on human consciousness and sub-consciousness.

As a consequence, such groups or individuals can no longer waste their energies of time, finance, service or information and revelation. To do so would be to have the energies withdrawn. They must send out freely, but all to whom they send must respond and complete the cycle. In this way both receiver and sender are strengthened and more energies are allowed to enter and to flow. For everything that goes forth, there must be a return of some nature. The return can take various forms. It can be financial, a true giving to help support the physical aspects of New Age unfoldment and a giving appropriate not only to meet needs but to make possible further expansion of service and work. The response can take place through an expression of gratitude to the human agency working at the source, as well as to God, and through a pledge to live the life suggested by the information or service sent out. It can consist of the willingness, through one's own efforts, to pass on what one receives in order to widen the reach of the flow. This is not done to further the power or influence of any one group or individual (which is why these energies are seeking to come through many) but to make it possible for the revelations and unfoldments of the New Age to come through and be established on as wide a foundation as possible. These energies will not and cannot be used for anyone's private benefit but only for the revealing and externalizing, for all men, of their inner, cosmic heritage of expanded consciousness. However, all who attune and live the life of these energies will receive benefit beyond all expectations.

Thus, no one may receive these energies who will not in some way contribute meaningfully to the whole and strengthen the flow of creativity and new life into human consciousness. That is the law. Pearls cannot be cast before time. These energies do not demand that people carry the word or the law to those unready to accept or unable to receive, nor to receive anything themselves that they do not wish for or cannot use, which would be wasteful and not the action of truth. However, it does demand that people strengthen the manifestation of the New Age through their own lives; they must be a living example of a New Age presence. It asks people to support and strengthen the links and activities of others who are truly manifesting that presence as well. If the example is well-lived, in joy, in love, in courage and confidence, then it will attract others.

Here is the fourth law: New Age energies can only flow where effort is made, in the individual or group life, to anchor these energies through living application. The New Age is not an intellectual exercise; it is not a spectator sport. Those whose consciousnesses are unwilling to work, to change, to shoulder the Light burden of externalizing through their own lives a dream and a cosmic heritage for mankind cannot receive these energies, for they would be wasted and would be an intolerable burden upon that individual. But those who prove in their lives the reality of these energies, who demonstrate the emerging of the New Age within, will receive more in increasing abundance. The day of study and retreat is past. We must balance our cerebrations and meditations with down-to-earth externalization and anchoring of the New Age visions.

These, then, are some of the laws that allow the energies of the New Age, energies of expanded power of consciousness, to enter and flow to man in safety and in cosmic balance. They form the body for a new heaven and a new earth. Now is the time to arise in consciousness and understanding in order to claim one's citizenship in the New and to pioneer a great and noble enterprise of world transformation and creation of a new civilization. It is not work for the weak but for those strong in inner living and outer manifestation, willing to receive these energies and obey the laws of their safe release. It is the call to live the God-inspired life of love, truth, service, discrimination and attunement.

From the vastnesses of man's inner potentials, as they are reflected to him through the Cosmic Presences now overlighting this world, these New Age energies are invoked. They come to deliver to man his unfoldment to heights undreamed. Yet they come with order, for such is their power and such is their love that the Cosmic Overlords who embody and channel these energies will not put man in jeopardy. Let us understand and use these laws as we hear and harken to the call. Then truly will we build as never before and man will emerge to his birthright of unlimited creativity and unity with God, the embodiment of law and the manifestor of a cosmic freedom.

Part III
Revelation:
The Cosmic and Personal Context

Chapter 11

The New Age

I am the Herald and the Truth of the New Age. I am new Revelation

A New Age . . . this is where we begin. This is the central concept from which all else stems. This is the supreme vision now: we are within a new dispensation, a new order of living and of consciousness. This is the essence of Revelation. The purpose of modern revelation is to place before men the reality and the characteristics of this New Age and to communicate to him the need to change in order to adapt successfully to these new characteristics. The New Age is a concept that proclaims a new opportunity, a new level of growth attained, a new power released and at work in human affairs, a new manifestation of that evolutionary tide of events which, taken at the flood, does indeed lead on to greater things, in this case to a new heaven, a new earth and a new humanity.

This is a powerful concept, one indeed worthy of the fullest and most powerful revelation. Yet, is it an accurate vision? Is there any truth behind calling this time in human history and world evolution the beginning of a New Age? Is the manifestation of various kinds of revelation throughout the world the only basis for proclaiming a New Age, or has something else truly happened which we need to recognize and understand and to which we need to adapt, hence the need for revelation to awaken us to this happening? This question of the validity and nature of the New Age concept needs to be answered first, for all else rests upon it.

The concept of classifying the evolution of life upon Earth as belonging to certain ages is not a new one. Geologists who study the strata of the earth's crust and paleontologists who investigate the fossilized remains of ancient creatures both speak of geological ages. The evolution of man's culture and civilizations is also categorized within "ages" when a certain kind of activity was prominent. Thus we have the Age of the Pyramids, the Dark Ages, the Age of Discovery, the Age of Reason, the Industrial Age and the Atomic Age. With the development of sophisticated machines and computers, many claim that we are now moving into a new age called the "Cybernetic Age", while others, pointing to man's leap into space, call this the Space Age.

Indeed, man's life on this planet has been transformed within the seventy years of this century into a veritable new age of advancing knowledge and technology. In less than sixty years, man advanced from the first powered air flight to a manned landing on the moon, an illustration of the almost incomprehensible acceleration to which human culture is being subjected. Looking to the future, it is projected that all human knowledge and information about the universe will double in the next ten years and double again in five years after that. Can we pretend that this will leave us unaffected? Can we not see that from this standpoint of technology and research alone we are entering a New Age and leaving forever the traditional patterns of human culture that existed before this time of atomics, genetic engineering, computers and space travel?

There is another reason, however, for calling this a New Age. It is found in Nature and revealed through the science of astronomy. It is due to a phenomenon of Earth's planetary motion known as the precession of the equinoxes. We can understand this if we imagine Earth as being the center of a vast celestial sphere. (*See diagram opposite.*) We know that the sun appears to move during the day from East to West and we also know that this apparent motion is really due to Earth's rotation on its axis. As Earth revolves around the sun once a year, it creates another apparent motion in which the sun moves along a circular path projected onto this celestial sphere. This path is called the ecliptic. Twelve constellations lie along this path, which is thus divided into twelve equal arcs. These constellations and the twelve arcs they form are called the zodiac. During the course of a year, the sun appears to move in a complete revolution through these twelve arcs or signs of the zodiac, though this motion is actually seen by an observer on Earth due to Earth's motion around the sun. You can easily illustrate this by walking around another person who is standing in the center of a room. He will appear to move against a changing background but it is you who are actually moving and thus changing your perspective of him and the background.

Because Earth is tilted on its axis, this ecliptic is not a perfectly horizontal path. If we imagine an equator on our celestial sphere, the ecliptic is seen as a circle slanting $23\frac{1}{2}°$ up and down from this equator at its highest and lowest points. The two points where the ecliptic crosses the celestial equator are called the equinoxes. This happens twice a year, creating the vernal (spring) equinox on March 21 and the autumnal equinox around September 22. On these days, the

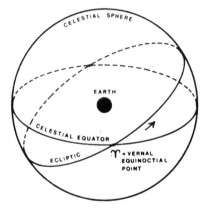

Apparent yearly motion of the sun among the stars is along the path of the ecliptic. Direction of the sun's apparent motion is indicated by arrow. The vernal equinoctial point appears to move in the opposite direction along the ecliptic.

length of the day and the night are equal, hence the name *equinox*.

The procession of the equinoxes is the retrograde or

backward motion of these equinoctial points along the ecliptic. The reason for this motion is involved with celestial and planetary mechanics which are not important here; the effect of this precession (which can be seen in a spinning top or gyroscope which not only rotates about an axis but has another motion in which the axis itself moves in a circle describing a cone in space) is to cause the equinoctial points to move backwards through the zodiac. They will describe a complete revolution about the ecliptic once in approximately 26,000 years. A little over 2100 years ago the vernal equinox could be projected onto the ecliptic at a point corresponding with the beginning of the constellation Aries. Then it moved backward into the arc of the constellation Pisces, creating a period of time known in astronomy and astrology as the Age of Pisces. Now the vernal equinoxtial point is leaving the constellation Pisces and entering the constellation of Aquarius. We enter the Age of Aquarius.

From this information, then, we see that Earth moves through twelve ages during the course of 26,000 years as the equinoctial points revolve around the ecliptic through each of the twelve zodiacal signs or arcs. We are now leaving one age and entering another; hence, the scientific basis for calling this a New Age. This motion of the equinoxes is due to actual celestial motion and changes in the relationship of Earth to its galactic environment. It is not far-fetched to assume that such changes may bring about the exposure of Earth and the life-streams upon it to differing energies from the cosmos. There is evidence of such changes in the past; the significance of entering a new arc on the ecliptic may well involve a deeper change than simply the motion of the equinox to face in a new celestial direction. Each position on the ecliptic, each zodiacal arc, may well expose Earth to subtle energies that manifest new and particular characteristics, affecting life and its evolution on this planet. Again, there is evidence beginning to be discovered suggesting that this is so, giving a deeper evolutionary meaning to the movement of the Earth through these ecliptic arcs, the twelve zodiacal ages, than merely that of being a cosmic calendar.

With this understanding that there is a scientific basis for calling this a New Age, just as there is a basis for calling January 1st a new year, we can probe more deeply into what the substance of this new cycle may be. For this, however, we must go further than a physically-oriented science can take us. To further our understanding of what this New Age represents we must seek concepts found through the awareness of a higher consciousness which is not limited by time or space. From such an expanded awareness, we can see the inner processes of change which add flesh to the mere skeleton of celestial motion; here we can see the drama of the evolution of consciousness which reveals the meaning and substance of the New Age. Grounded on the astronomical validity of proclaiming a New Age, we can explore the spiritual validities which give to that proclamation substance and implications fully worthy of a new Revelation.

We are considering the cosmic context of this Revelation. The aspect of the cosmos which most concerns us here is the solar system. From the standpoint of expanded consciousness, what is the solar system? Far more than a collection of planets revolving around a sun, it is the manifestation of the Life and characteristics of a highly evolved Being, known in the mystery teachings as the Solar Logos. This is, in itself, a revelation to many people who are accustomed to thinking in purely physical terms of animate and inanimate life, but it has been known by mystics and pioneers of advanced consciousness throughout the centuries that all the universe is alive and everything is the manifestation of some form of living Intelligence. Now, as part of the revelations of the New Age, this knowledge is being spread more widely. More importantly, it is being proven by concrete demonstrations of contact, communion and co-operation with the various levels of life within and beyond the physical level of manifestation, as in the story of the Findhorn garden.

The solar system is the creative manifestation of the Solar

Logos. It was created partly because of the joy which all living beings know when they are expressing themselves through their Divine heritage of creativity and accomplishment. On the other hand, it also represents a service on the part of this great Being to other lives which have yet to expand his level of action and awareness. The solar system is an environment within which these less developed lives can learn and grow and expand in their creative powers and the release of their indwelling creative potentials. Creation is not a static condition. New creation is always springing forth as new revelations and aspects of God, the Divine Whole, are unfolded by the continuously developing creativity of living beings on many levels of consciousness.

The Solar Logos does not work alone in creating such an environment of educational possibilities as the solar system represents. Other great lives are attracted to him through their attunement to his purposes and ideals; not so highly developed as he, they nonetheless are evolved enough that their lives and consciousnesses can be the centers around which can develop those specific environments of life and opportunity we call the planets. Such a Being is the one who is the source of energy and direction for the manifestation of Earth, the life for whom Earth is the body. This one is called the Earth Logos.

There are other helpers, as well, for the Solar Logos and the various Planetary Logos. These include beings whose function is to provide the order and direction through their highly evolved consciousnesses within which the vast currents of energy and power can flow between the planets and the sun and the cosmos beyond, both in a physical way and within the inner realms of higher dimensional expression. Each planet also has its complements of cosmically attuned beings who serve the development and well-being of the planet and create the proper environment for physical or etheric life to evolve within. These beings act throughout the entire scheme of Nature and are occultly known as the Devas and the Elementals.

All of these beings, from the Solar Logos on down to the simplest Elemental life upon a planet, work to provide an educational environment for the cultivation, nourishment and expansion of the Divine life-streams using the solar system and its planets as their "schoolhouse". The whole solar system, from the physical level on up to the cosmically oriented levels of the awareness of the Solar Logos, is like a womb in which seeds of consciousness develop and unfold into a full flowering of that unobstructed awareness and creativity that is the God-life and cosmic consciousness inherent within all creation. At that point, these consciousnesses, full-fledged beings of radiant creative Divinity, go forth as graduates of this solar system into the infinite universe beyond to become, in turn, educators for the life-streams following after them and seeds for still greater manifestations of God-life yet to unfold from the potentials within Divine Mind.

The method of stimulating and directing this evolutionary process is one of exposing consciousness to various kinds of energy which express themselves through appropriate experiences, such as an experience of love exposes an individual to the energy of love. Such exposure has an educational effect in that it "leads out" from within the consciousness an awareness and manifestation of the corresponding energy lying dormant within that consciousness. In this way, the being learns to recognize and to externalize what is within itself by having the essence of its inner nature reflected back and revealed to it through experiences in its environment.

Ultimately, there is no separation between the "inner" and the "outer", the microcosm within an individual and the macrocosm of his environment. All the characteristics of life expressed by the Solar Logos are inherent within all beings who share and draw upon that life. In a greater degree, all energies and characteristics inherent in the universe beyond are also potential within the Solar Logos, if not actually being expressed, and thus are inherent in all who share his life. Thus, every being shares, in the microcosm of his individual aspect of Divinity, the essential characteristics found throughout all the Divinely created cosmos. As he is exposed to these characteristics functioning in his environment, he learns to recognize them and to work with them, which teaches him to recognize them within himself. He is then stimulated to externalize and express these characteristics, uniting the microcosm of his individual Divinity with the macrocosm of the universal God. When this is accomplished, he moves into a new environment or is exposed to new energies and characteristics and the educational process is repeated, though now on a higher level.

The educational environment in which this evolution occurs is represented and governed by the energies (and the great beings that control such energies through their consciousnesses) to which an individual is exposed. He is to recognize his oneness with them and learn to use these energies creatively and in harmony with the whole of life through the vehicle of his individuality. When he does this, the environment changes as new energies enter to provide new opportunities for growth. He then must change and adapt to what these new energies represent. This process is true for the evolution of human consciousness, planetary consciousness and even, on his vast level, for the Solar Logos, who is himself still evolving. Any change which affects the evolution of the Solar Logos affects, in turn, all the lives that share his life; the energies that come from cosmic levels to educate him have an educative effect on all lives within the solar system. They create a change which all must meet and to which all must adapt. Such a change occurs approximately every 2100 years.

This is the inner significance to the precession of the equinoxes and is the true validity for proclaiming a New Age. Though there are lesser and greater cycles of individual, planetary and solar change, there are these twelve cycles in each of which new energies are received and the energies that represented the "lesson material" for the previous cycle are generally phased out. We enter the Age of Aquarius through the movement of the vernal equinox into that sign on the ecliptic. With this comes a change of energy and a new stimulus to the continuing unfoldment of the creative Divinity within the entire solar family. This is the true New Age: a cyclic event within the education of the solar system, an outpouring of new revelations of the nature of Divine Life within all things and a call to the inherent spirit moving within form and matter to match these revelations with recognition of their corresponding presence within the evolving being. Out of such recognition comes the externalization of new life, new consciousness, new behaviour, new power, new creativity that will transform the outer and inner environment of that spirit and truly bring into manifestation the characteristics and phenomena that will reveal a new heaven, a new earth and a New Age.

Chapter 12

The Foundations of Revelation

Revelation is the process through which the New Age is making itself known to humanity. It is a dynamic process of unfoldment from the unknown wombs of the infinite of a new life; it is the process of externalizing the characteristics of the New Age from within through living this new life. Revelation is far more than words, far more than an event. It is a continuing process of unfoldment, of education. What we are calling revelation is specifically that unfoldment of the characteristics of the Age of Aquarius, but revelation has always been with us. Whenever and wherever learning and growth and evolution take place, there is the revelation of new talents, new powers, new possibilities.

The revelation of this New Age, the process of unfolding the new energies of the Aquarian cycle and making them known, began first on the level of the Solar Logos as he adjusted his consciousness to receive and adapt to new characteristics of Divine energy. A change on his part affects all life within the solar system. Hence, the process of revelation moved down to the level of the Planetary Logoi, creating the necessity for a comparable change and expansion on their parts in order to receive and benefit from this new outpouring.

This is a new revelation. It unfolds energies and opportunities and characteristics of consciousness new on Earth. Yet, it is not a sudden nor an unexpected event. The foundations of revelation are sunk deep into the history of Earth and the evolution of human consciousness. This New Age has been foreseen for centuries by individuals who had learned to manifest a cosmic consciousness and could witness, freed from time and space, the unfolding patterns of development for life on this planet. They saw what this New Age would bring as the logical continuance of the unfoldment of creative being, an important phase in the curriculum of consciousness. They also saw what prior development and preparation would be needed by evolving life, humanity in particular, in order properly to receive and benefit from the energies and opportunities the New Age would bring. With this knowledge, these great ones began to prepare the consciousness of mankind and of all the world.

What was their vision of the need? Towards what ends was this preparation directed? For humanity, it was seen that the Aquarian cycle would stimulate the emergence of a new kind of consciousness, an intuitive-mental awareness, attuned to a level of knowing and power unlimited by space and time. Such a consciousness would have its creative faculties greatly enhanced. This would be in contrast to the emotional-mental awareness within which man has functioned for many centuries, an awareness very much bounded by concepts of separation, time and space and thus comparatively limited in its creative powers. The unleashing of greater creativity without comparable change in the level of man's awareness and direction would be like placing weapons in the hands of children. Because of the scope of the new powers which New Age consciousness offers to man, these abilities can only be exercised within an environment of love, selflessness and a sensitive dedication to and awareness of the good of the whole of life. Without such a consciousness of love and that sensitive discrimination between what is appropriate in the moment and what is not (a sensitivity known as truth), these energies and the powers they would stimulate cannot be released. Therefore, it was necessary to do everything possible to unfold and nourish from humanity at least the strong seeds, if not an actual blossoming, of such a consciousness of love and truth.

Against this need was seen the reality of the challenge of physical form life, a challenge that is a unique part of the educational environment which the Earth Logos provides. Much of the special evolution which Earth stimulates is in learning to deal with dense conditions of energy, learning the creative possibilities of limitation while, at the same time, learning how to transcend limitation, still maintaining the link with those possibilities. This requires the spiritual Being who seeks such evolution to express through a physical body. This would be impossible if it were not for the action of certain forces of materialization which "weigh" the Being down, adding the element of gravity to his vibrational expression. Diving provides an analogy to this. To overcome the natural buoyancy of the body which would not permit him to sink below a certain level, a diver wears weights. However, if he uses too much weight he has difficulty in rising again, which could be fatal.

In a like manner, if a consciousness becomes too involved with the energies of gravity and materialization, the forces that pull downward into density, then it runs the risk of not being able to rise again properly. It becomes increasingly aligned with these involutionary energies which transform its spiritual nature into one more closely attuned to material energy. If this process were not checked, such a consciousness could eventually fall from its higher vibratory level to become permanently a part of the realm of matter. For an evolving consciousness this would be disastrous.

The fall of man was the original alignment of his spiritual energies with these forces of materialization so that he could enter into physical experience. Though this represented a sacrifice in some respects, yet it prepared the way for a more expanded expression of his spirit once he had graduated from the curriculum of creative density. However, mankind began becoming too involved with the energies and beings of materialization and began running the risk of becoming too entrapped in the realms of matter and form. Then, when the time came for his consciousness to grasp and receive energies stimulating his higher faculties and lifting him back into the realm of spirit as a Master of Evolution, a time represented by this New Age, he would be unable to rise accordingly. The whole evolutionary process would be thrown out of schedule, slowed down and possibly even thwarted. Again, in analogy, it would be like a diver who had entered the depths in search of

116

treasure. Having found it, he waited for the rope to be lowered from his boat on the surface above, in order that he might tie this rope to the treasure, allowing both him and it to be lifted back up. Then he discovered that, intent on his treasure seeking, he had gone too deep and the rope couldn't reach him. Man, too, was about his task of gathering the treasure of experience but he was becoming so focussed on this that he was forgetting his true home in the higher levels and was going too deep into matter and density. His character was increasingly reflecting the characteristics of matter which are separation, rigidity, conflict and intertia and he was ceasing to manifest the higher qualities of an uplifting Love, Truth and balanced Wisdom.

Needless to say, evolving consciousness is not exposed to such a challenge without help being present in the form of counterbalancing energies. The counterbalances to involution and gravity are evolution and education, the processes of leading out and freeing the powers of life hidden within. The force that governs all education in the universe, the uplifting force, the energy that continually acts like a leaven throughout evolution, the universal Presence that calls out of form and spirit the higher potentials of Divine life waiting to be released into expression, is the Christ.

There are no words to express truly or fully the nature and work and splendour of that universal Presence men have called the Christ. He is the motive power behind all evolution and he is the product of that evolution. He stands revealed in the macrocosm and calls forth to himself within the microcosm; he hears this call and comes forth, revealing himself again to the universe and calling forth again to that which he is still within the microcosms of lesser evolved life-streams. Thus it goes throughout evolution. He is the point, the goal, the Life that calls all to himself and he is the Life within all that responds and arises.

The Christ is the essence of all evolving life; he lives within all. Thus, when the Earth Logos became the centre of creative consciousness around which the planet could form, the Christ was intimately a part of this creative process. From the Christ Life of the Logos down to the Christ Life of the simplest pebble or organism, he was present in the foundations of Earth. Once this planet had been formed, then it was bathed in the educational energies — the first "lessons" — designed to unfold this Christ potential from all the lives using Earth as their schoolhouse. These energies came from the Cosmic Christ, the educator for this solar system and indeed for all the universe.

The process is for the Christ to "stand" outside of the educational environment of the planet and to "call" the evolving life to arise, to come forth and to return to him bearing the treasures of experience and learning. This is a physical way of picturing it and it must be realized that this is an oversimplication to describe a process occurring beyond the limitations of finite mind. With that reservation, though, it is useful as a parable of what happened next. The evolutionary process on Earth decrees involvement with the forces of materialization. The Christ energies, from the higher levels of Being, bathed the planet and the evolving lives struggled to respond, but within the realms of Earth the materialistic energies were the most apparent and hence had the most impact on awakening consciousness. This consciousness, particularly within the human expression, most frequently attuned to these energies. While they are not evil, the forces of materialization cannot assist consciousness to assimilate experience and turn it into that uplifting force of Wisdom. These forces can only give the consciousness repeated experience of a certain kind without providing any true educational or integrating power that would enable the life to arise into greater levels of Wholeness. The energies of matter eventually overwhelm the consciousness with apparently endless experiences of the most limited cause-and-effect kind and, by increasing the sense of separation and disintegration, ultimately deaden that consciousness.

It was against this tremendous downward pull, necessary on the one hand, yet becoming out of balance on the other, that the Cosmic Christ sought to contend through his outpourings of Spiritual Life, Love, Light and Truth. He could not interfere directly, since to do so would be to deprive the evolving life-streams of their chance to grow through learning to provide within themselves the counterbalance to the materialistic forces. Great beings came to Earth to assist as teachers and enlighteners but they, too, were limited since they were not part of the evolutionary stream of Earth. It was necessary for an agent of Earth to reach a point where he could link with the Cosmic Christ and radiate his energies. So the more highly evolved members of the human kingdom worked to attain this goal.

Finally, one individual succeeded. He fully awakened to this energy, contacted it and became one with the Cosmic Christ. He became known as the Buddha, the Enlightened or Awakened One. Outwardly, he presented the teachings for the age in which he lived, demonstrating the necessary principle of truth as it expresses through a sensible discrimination and balance. His teachings were important to that stage of human evolution and also prepared the way for the teachings that were to come in the future. Yet, the real impact of his life and triumph was felt on the inner subjective levels of Earth. For, as he arose in consciousness and awoke to the Presence of the Cosmic Christ, there was released throughout all Earth evolution (since he himself was part of that evolution) a corresponding vibration of stimulation and arising and awakening. This obeys the principle that the success of one individual affects the whole of life to which he belongs and uplifts the whole. As the Buddha established, through his own consciousness and life, the link with the Cosmic Christ, this link was shared with all evolving Earth lives. Over the centuries this link was strengthened between the Cosmic Christ and the planetary consciousness of man; through it, the cosmic energies of upliftment were able to come into closer and closer relationship with Earth. It was as if man had been on one side of a chasm of consciousness and the Christ had been on the other and the Buddha had built a bridge between. Since most men were still unable to cross to his side, the Christ began to cross to their side in order to join mankind. As he and his energy approached from the higher levels of consciousness, sensitive men and women knew that a great event was portending. The prophets, struggling to convey the nature of this event, spoke of a Coming, a Birth and a Saviour.

Two thousand years ago the vernal equinox was moving into the constellation Pisces and the Piscean Age was beginning. As part of this zodiacal rhythm, new energies were sweeping into action over the consciousnesses of Earth, energies of love and devotion and idealism. Using these energies as a vehicle, the Cosmic Christ completed "crossing the bridge" and also began his blending with the evolutionary life of earth. At this time, another individual awoke fully to the reality of this Cosmic Presence. Like the Buddha, he became enlightened, awakened to the Christ within himself. He began to live and express this indwelling Christ Consciousness, externalizing it into loving service to his world. Unlike the Buddha, this individual went a step further. Through the vibrational quality and power of his consciousness, he became at one with the Cosmic Christ and became the focal point for the descent and anchoring upon Earth of this greater life and energy. Thus, Jesus became the Annointed One, the Christos, anointed with the downpouring Light, love, life and power of the Cosmic Christ.

Then began one of the greatest dramas of this planet's history, the impregnation of an aspect of the Cosmic Christ, through the consciousness of Jesus, into the physical, etheric and spiritual life of Earth. Jesus gave the teachings of love and compassion demanded by his age, but on the inner subjective levels the true drama and ministry was consummated. Jesus had awakened to the Christ of his own nature. Through living that Christ and externalizing it, he attuned to the descending Cosmic Christ and opened the gate through his own consciousness for this greater energy of Divinity to be born on the earth plane and to relate to mankind directly, a

120

mankind unable to contact him in any other way, for it had lost touch with its own higher levels of Being.

However, the Cosmic Christ did not come only for humanity, but in service to all evolving life-streams of all the kingdoms of Nature upon the planet. Through the channel made for him by the human consciousness of Jesus, the Christ entered the very structure and life of Earth and united with his counterpart within the Earth Logos. An aspect of Cosmic Life and Power, a seed, was planted. From this seed-point, the educational, stimulating power of the Cosmic Christ could radiate from within Earth itself; it was as if Earth and all upon it had become radioactive with a new life. Part of the Life, Awareness and Power of the Cosmic Christ became incarnated into Earth, not to be released until the evolution of the Lives of Earth could attune to him and release this Life back to Its cosmic homeland. This was the occult crucifixion, the placing of this Cosmic Presence within the cross of matter, space and time, laying the Christ within the tomb of a level of life expression of great density by his standards. There he would stay until the Ascension of Consciousness would take place in the life-streams of the planet, especially those of the human kingdom.

Through this action of sacrifice, the Cosmic Christ truly became a Saviour. Now he no longer "stood outside" the evolution of Earth; he had entered that evolution Himself, incarnated within it, become part of it, accepted its limitations. From that point he could influence this evolution directly. Operating within the etheric structure of Earth, that level which is the source of all energy for physical manifestation, he had far more power to offset the momentum of the materialistic energies which had been building upon Earth through the consciousness of mankind. To return to our earlier analogy, he could stop the diver from going too far down, unable to rise. He was a force of effervescence, of upliftment dynamically active within the life of Earth, able more effectively to counterbalance and transcend the spiritual effects of gravity, the downward pull on consciousness. He was a Saviour indeed, adding new buoyancy to all life and giving a renewed impetus toward the realization by all life of the eternally indwelling presence of the Christ and its power within.

Throughout the past twenty centuries, the seed of cosmic energy and Life implanted into the womb of Earth has been germinating, gathering strength within the etheric levels of being. The demonstration of Jesus's life worked preparing the soil of men's hearts and minds, giving to them an ideal that calls forth a dedication, a love, a compassion and sensitivity and self-sacrifice unheard of previously. Behind this outer activity, this seed of regeneration has been establishing itself as an increasingly powerful center of radiating Cosmic Life, steadily transforming the inner life of Earth. It has been creating a sensitivity and a receptiveness on the etheric level that would be vital to receive the new energies of the Aquarian cycle, energies designed to raise Earth and all upon it into a higher level of attunement to universal life. Thus, on outer planes through the activity of men and women living the example that Jesus set and on inner levels through the transforming, regenerating power of this growing seed of Christ life, the preparation for the New Age moved forward.

This work of preparation was vital, for without it, as we have seen, the lives evolving upon Earth would not be able to receive the outpourings of the New Age. It is a key to understanding the Revelation of Limitless Love and Truth. It is based on a simple principle, that of the lock and the key. The key and lock must be mated to each other, that is, they must fit if there is to be a fulfilment of their function. Likewise, currents of new energies must enter a situation that can use and handle those energies properly if fusion and perfect fulfilment, in the form of growth and new creation, are to manifest. Another analogy for this is in the installation of electrical wiring. If the Electric Company comes to link up the circuits of your house with the main lines and you have all the proper wiring completed and the sockets and outlets available, then all is well. However, if you are not ready when the cables from the main lines are brought to you, then, at the least, you delay the operation and you may have to wait before the electricity men come back again. On the other hand, you may create a situation of danger. You would be unprepared to channel such current safely or constructively and you might electrocute yourself in the presence of an exposed live wire. This would be an evil situation, for evil is basically the manifestation of a force that is out of place or out of timing, inappropriate to the needs and realities of the situation. Just as the men from the Electric Company would not expose you to such dangers as live wires, so the higher Beings who control the cosmic energies will not create an evil situation; rather than release their powers to consciousnesses unready for them, they will withdraw. Thus, there was the necessity for preparation upon the outer and within the inner planes of the etheric to make the consciousnesses of Earth ready to receive these energies properly when the time came.

This etheric level of Earth, as I am using the term here, represents the level of consciousness and energy wherein operate those formative forces whose activities bring all physical forms into existence and maintain them in physical existence. It is like a mould which sets the patterns into which and about which energy can crystallize into dense physical matter. Change the mould and you change the physical manifestation; control the mould and likewise you control the physical manifestation. It is obviously a plane of great power. It is like a great transformer. It receives powerful energies of life and creativity from solar and cosmic sources and transforms these energies into forms which can manifest as physical density. All nuclear energy is rooted in this more basic etheric level of energy; the power that sustains the physical atom in existence comes from the etheric. This level is very susceptible to influence from consciousness. It can be influenced by "feedback" coming from the physical plane of manifestation or, more powerfully, it can be influenced by energies coming from the levels of emotion or mind, or from spiritual levels beyond.

To picture this more clearly, we shall simplify the nature of the etheric plane and imagine that it has two characteristics, the one being reflective, the other being receptive and formative. In the first case, it is like a mirror, relfecting the forms, the feelings and emotions and the thoughts that emanate from the physical plane and from man's activities primarily, since the consciousness of mankind is the most powerful acting on the physical level. Thus, everything has its etheric counterpart and this level of the etheric plane, which may be likened to the "bottom" level closest to the physical, reflects the earth in all its aspects: physical, emotional and mental. Here are found recorded the images of past actions and activity and the images of present patterns.

The formative level of the etheric is the creative level. It does not reflect images of the past or present; it receives creative impulses from Spirit and moulds itself accordingly, whether that spirit is functioning on non-physical levels or whether it is incarnating. This level of the etheric reflects the future and establishes the moulds into which and around which energies may crystallize into physical form. The reflective ether mirrors the forms of yesterday and today. The formative ether holds the images of forms that will exist tomorrow. It is the essence of "faith", which is "the substance of things unseen." When you project an idea of something you would like, it takes shape and form on this formative etheric according to the power and clarity of your thought and desire. As you accept the reality of this unseen form, it takes on life and will precipitate itself into physical form. This is the essence of the laws of manifestation.

These two characteristics of the etheric are not absolutely separate; they influence each other. The patterns of the past can affect the development of the future; because the known is always more powerful in men's minds than the unknown, the images of the past in the reflective etheric generally have more power than the images of cration and of a new future in the formative ethers. They can prevent the proper development of such new creativity. This is why so much energy usually has to be expended by pioneers and creators to get their ideas into form, for they are fighting the inertia of past thinking mirrored on the reflective etheric.

The etheric is like the lock; the energies of new life, new transformation, new lessons are the key that unlocks the creative powers of this level and reveals new opportunities. However, if the key and the lock don't fit, then nothing happens. Another analogy is that of the Electric Company. The etheric is like the wiring of the house waiting to receive new power from the universal mains; if the wiring is inappropriate to the incoming power, danger results.

Because of the power of the thinking and feeling of mankind, the reflective etheric, which mirrors the quality and form of such thought and emotion, is equally powerful. Its characteristics dominate the flow and quality and direction of energy throughout the etheric level. The thinking and feeling of man have been notoriously filled with conflict, destruction, confusion, fear, hatred, separation and a spiritual gravity and alignment with materializing forces; hence, these are the qualities that strongly influence the nature of etheric energy. The energies of the New Age include forces that stimulate and strengthen the formative etheric; they stimulate manifestation. Whatever is held on inner, subjective levels of consciousness develops an increased tendency to crystallize out into objective, usually physical, manifestation. If the reflections of man's anguished thinking and emotion were more powerfully precipitated into physical plane reality, it would be appalling. Further, many of the energies of the New Age are highly constructive. They cannot flow through "wires" that are destructive in their direction. Hence, these energies could not enter the etheric life of Earth if destruction, suffering, hatred, separation and so forth were the dominant patterns there. Yet, if the etheric planes of Earth do not receive these energies, then the physical planes of manifestation cannot receive them, for all must flow through the etheric. Thus, the negative characteristics of the etheric plane formed a barrier against the manifestation of the New Age and its qualities of powerful new life and creativity.

For the "lock" of the etheric to fit the "key" of the New Age, for the "wiring" to be fit to receive the powerful currents of stimulation which Aquarius would bring, the etheric level of Earth had to have a dominant consciousness and life of love, truth, wisdom, order and stability — the pattern of the Christ. The life of Christ had to be the life active within the etheric body of the Earth Logos, successfully counteracting the materializing forces that were increasing the flow of negative energy upon Earth. The Earth Logos had to experience the birth of a more powerful Christ life within himself, a transformation, a regeneration, a rebirth of his Spirit.

Having been introduced and anchored within Earth by the life and ministry of Jesus, the Cosmic Christ, operating from the seed-point of his life impregnated within Earth, set about to accomplish this rebirth, the development of a new etheric pattern powerful enough to offset the negative projections of human consciousness and pure enough to receive the outpourings of the New Age. He would stimulate and build around the seed-concept of Limitless Love and Truth, as demonstrated by Jesus and the Buddha, a new mould of life and power and light. From this would develop the new etheric body of the Earth Logos.

Gradually, silently, this mould and this body have been built up, drawing for its energies upon the arising consciousness of men and women throughout the world who have responded to the ideas of love, truth and wisdom and have released these creative energies by living lives attuned to these ideas. It has been a secret project, deeply hidden and unheralded, lest these sacred energies be diverted or tapped wrongly or ahead of schedule. As men were taught by the advanced souls of the race to open their hearts and minds and live in love and trust, behind the scenes, in the creative womb of Earth's consciousness, a new life was developing and preparing for its birth.

This is the foundation for modern Revelation. It is a deep foundation, sunk into the centuries of striving, by human consciousness of all cultures and races and religions, to attune to the highest impulses within mankind and to release the infinite powers of creativity and joy contained within him. This preparation for Aquarius is a tremendous operation. There was the operation of the "Saviour-Christ" whose force of Light and Love and Truth contested the powers of darkness and worked to cleanse the emotional and mental planes of those energies and thought-forms of limitation which had been born of the union of man and the materialistic energies. This cleansing aided the educational process of drawing out from man, through examples of great men and women, his powers of higher thought and attunement and control of his emotional pattern. There were also presented to him the spiritual ideas of love, faith, truth and wisdom expressed at the heart of all religions, ideas important to future development. And behind all this outer activity of cleansing, stimulation and education, the great work of the Cosmic Christ and the Earth Logos went steadily forward, the work of building the foundations for revelation, the frame and body of a new heaven and a new earth for rebirth into a New Age.

Chapter 13

A New Heaven and a New Earth

I form the center, a cosmic seed-atom, for the building of a new heaven and a new earth. I am the new heaven and the new earth. I unfold from within [the planet] what it has always stored there and which shall form the new. [I draw] to Me the elements that will form the new heaven and the new earth. . . . The new heaven and the new earth are forming in your midst.

How is a planet born? Is it in the fiery heart of cosmic gases swirling together, drawn together down a gravity well until their free-flowing energies become locked in the intimate embrace that is matter? Or is its birth in a deeper, more powerful realm, a womb of consciousness where the desire and the image can grow together and build until they form the creative Idea, the seed-atom, around which the energies can crystallize and take form? Within the etheric formative levels are the energies that empower creative manifestation. All that is needed is the spark of an Idea to set these creative forces aflame. This is the birthplace of a world: consciousness, the consciousness that conceives the Image, the Idea, and fires the spark that alights the etheric planes into magnetic formative activity. Then all that is needed is drawn to this centre to cloak the Idea in form and make it an expressed reality instead of a potential.

How is a planet reborn? How does a new world emerge? On a smaller scale, how is a man who has passed through his mother's womb born again? It is in consciousness, the level of true Being and power. It is done through the power of a living Idea, a concept that draws to itself what it needs to give itself form and reality. It draws from the growth and promise and potentials of the past, and from the visions and hopes of the future, and from the soil of what is and what has been; it gives birth to the transforming blossom of what may be and shall be. The new is given life and form.

Once the original birth has taken place, all subsequent rebirths really represent the further unfolding of qualities potentially inherent in the Being or Idea. Under the educational impact of the Christ, which draws out these potentials and gives them reality, new unfoldment and new manifestations occur which seem like rebirths. Yet this manifestation did exist previously, if unseen and unrealized.

It is this way in the birth and rebirth of a man. The seed of the father and of the mother contain all the possibilities for new form, possibilities which are realized along a certain direction when the two are joined. The child develops as a blended form expressing the characteristics inherited from paternal and maternal streams of life. It also uses these characteristics to develop and express its own unique identity. Within that identity may be hidden talents and potentials which are unrealized until one day he encounters a living force, an idea or a vision expressed through some other person or situation which sparks these hidden talents to life. When this happens, he experiences a change of consciousness and personality under the impact of this unfoldment from within; it is not at all uncommon for the physical environment in which he lives to change, as well, in correspondence to the inner change. He may seek new employment, move to a new habitat, change his friends as his interests and direction change. Eventually, he may look back upon his past and recognize that that experience had been a turning point. He may wonder how he could ever have been the way he was before it had happened to him. Yet, as we have seen, even before this change he had held as potentials the characteristics which, when brought to the surface, brought about the change. His rebirth came in consciousness first, then all else in his life adjusted into new patterns accordingly.

This same pattern is followed in the inner work of the Cosmic Christ and the Earth Logos. Within the heart of Earth lay the potentiality of Limitless Love and Truth, Light and power, characteristics which the life-streams upon Earth will continue to develop and express in the course of their evolution. Yet, this evolution was challenged by other forces which, though important in the role and educational function of the planet, threatened, through imbalance, to shift the direction of life into unproductive conditions. A rebirth, a fresh release of new purpose and direction, was necessary to correct this. Earth needed to be born again, to manifest a new consciousness and a new life.

The Christ is eternally the agent of rebirth throughout creation. He is the universal power and life that prevents stagnation, that invokes and nourishes growth and continuous unfoldment. He unites with the consciousness of what is and what has been and through that union gives birth to the consciousness of what can be and shall be. He reveals the hidden splendours and gives them release into the freedom of expression. The life of the new is the life of the old that has been transformed, through some degree of union with the Christ, into a greater fulfillment and expansion. The life of the old is the foundation on which the new is built; it is the seed from which unfold new stages of creative being. In the presence of the Christ, the past and the future become fused lovingly, creatively into the reality of manifestation in the living Now.

Thus, the Cosmic Christ united with the consciousness of the Earth Logos in which were sunk the foundations of Earth and its past development and future potentials. Through that union, a seed-atom of Christ-power began to radiate within the inner spheres of Earth, summoning forth the beginnings of a new consciousness for Earth: a new revelation, a rebirth through the realization of the potentials for a new heaven, which would correspondingly create a new earth of forms to express this new consciousness.

There are two creative sources upon Earth. Ideally, they should be one, but in history they have rarely been so. The primary source is the consciousness of the Earth Logos. From him come the ideas, the visions which are built upon by those spiritual intelligences known as the Devas and Elementals, to create the etheric and physical environments of Nature within which life can thrive and evolve. From the Earth Logos there also proceeds that empowering and sustaining energy which, arising through etheric levels, enters the material world as the nuclear energy that creates and maintains the physical atom in existence. Thus, the life and consciousness of the Earth Logos is active etherically within every atomic nucleus, supporting all physical existence.

The second creative source is man and his consciousness. He is the only Being on Earth who shares the God-power of ideation and imagination, the ability to form ideas, visions, images and to invoke the energies necessary to materialize these into form. This is because man is truly made in God's creative image; he is essentially a cosmic, spiritual Being who is sojourning within physical form to learn to use his creativity wisely and effectively. Because he is a Son of God, man has the ability to attune consciously and with self-knowing to the presence of the Divine and to hold an awareness of that flow and direction of the Whole of life which we call the will of God. He can then use his developing powers of creativity to assist this flow to fulfill itself properly.

On the other hand, man can attune primarily to the materializing powers, in which case his consciousness tends to take on the characteristics of form, which are limitation and separation. He becomes isolated within his own personal patterns, attuned only to his own wishes and desires and goals. He still has the creative power of materialization (though fortunately limited by his form-oriented mind) but what he creates in this case will reflect the narrowness and limitation of his vision. It will most likely be tangent to the proper flow, out of timing and out of place (which is the definition I am using of a negative or evil force). He sees the world not through the eyes of the Whole of life, the vision of God, but through his self-oriented personal vision. He sees the world as it should be to him as a personality. From this he creates his private world, giving it form and reality in the world at large through the actions and attitudes of his life.

In this manner, there exist several earths. There is the ecological earth, the body of the Earth Logos and the creation of his consciousness and love. This is the earth from which man derives all his nourishment and substance, however much he may forget this fact. Then there is the private earth that exists only in the thoughts and feelings of each individual human being. It is the way he or she sees the world and from this vision develops his or her personal goals and direction. Out of these billions of little world-views, as they are blended by culture and civilization, emerges the thought-form of the earth which is the product of man's thinking as a species. Where this world-view is similar or identical to the characteristics and direction of the flow of ecological earth, harmony results. Where they are different, conflict is usually evident and man and Nature are seen as being at odds with each other.

Revelation is the unfoldment of the direction in which the evolution of life is moving, according to the will of God. The Earth Logos naturally is in harmony with this will and directs his life accordingly, as do all his helpers within Nature. This is not sufficient if the direction man chooses to travel is at a tangent or even in opposition to this flow of the Whole. Therefore, Revelation, the birth of a new heaven and a new earth, cannot occur only on the inner planes of consciousness and life, though it must begin there. It must be matched by a complementary revelation and rebirth within the creative consciousness of mankind. Otherwise, the gap would widen between the real world that proceeds from the life of the Earth Logos and the thought-form world created by man's consciousness. This would only increase tension between these two sources of creative power and release increasingly destructive forces of conflict. In any such contest, man would be hopelessly out-classed, for in spite of all his power, he is still dependent on the ecological earth for his substance. If he disrupts that ecology or separates himself from it or is in aggressive conflict with it, the probable result will be his being overwhelmed by an outraged and unsympathetic Nature.

Therefore, complementary Births had to take place, one with the consciousness of Earth, one within the consciousness of man, in order to unite these two creative streams into a unified flow and direction and co-operative unfoldment. On the other hand, the Cosmic Christ incarnated within the etheric structure of Earth, as we have seen, establishing there a center of his power and life which would grow to become the body of a new heaven and a new earth. At the same time, the Christ, acting within the consciousness of Jesus and others who could attune to and share that Christhood, entered the stream of human thought and feeling and history. There he gave new life and power to the ideas of love, truth, service, compassion and wisdom and inspired men and women to give these Ideas strength and permanency through their living example of them. Thus, within individual consciousness and within the collective consciousness of mankind, these ideas germinated to form the conceptual basis for a new humanity to live upon the new earth.

This is an important concept. Just as the foundations of Revelation have existed in the inner spheres of Earth, so have they existed within the personal development of each of us throughout the ages. Just as the embryo of a new world has grown within the heart of the Earth Logos, nourished and stimulated by the intimate presence of the Christ, so the embryo of a new world of personal consciousness has been developing comparably within the inner being of each individual. Even for us, the New Age and the revelation heralding it are not sudden or unexpected events but ones for which we, too, have been preparing for at least two thousand years and generally for longer. Nourished by the lives and examples of saints and seers and great men and women of all cultures and races, the ideas of love and truth and wise and powerful service have been held before mankind. However much the outer personality might ignore or even contest these ideas, the individual life could not escape being exposed to them or influenced by them in some fashion. So, through such exposure and influence, there has been growing in each of us a New Age body, an inner body of Light and love, embryonic and potential but nonetheless real, awaiting the call of the New Age to bring it forth into expression.

It is a spiritual phenomenon that coming events cast their shadows before them. Easily two hundred years before the actual beginning of a new age, the energies that will characterize it begin to be felt. The patterns of the old cycle are agitated in anticipation as, deep within them, the unexpressed potentials that will become realized in the succeeding age begin to move to the surface. Often this produces "false labors," manifestations which reflect the coming of the real birth but which are premature. Over the past two centuries, man's prophetic nature often proclaimed itself as he sensed these anticipations. False labors appeared from the womb of man's consciousness. New religious movements sprang up around the world in anticipation of the Second Coming or of new revelation, and new messiahs proclaimed themselves with regularity. Often these movements held great value in themselves and added much to enriching man's consciousness, but in their identification with a new birth, they were out of timing. Often only disappointment and disillusionment followed some of the more spectacular movements which promised the immanent arrival of the millenium, but the energies of expectancy and renewed faith which focused the thoughts and emotions of people onto the spiritual worlds of life and onto the possibility of new revelation, added strength to the true embryos of Revelation growing within the twin wombs of the earth and man. Such false labors served to keep the concept of the birth of a new heaven and a new earth alive in the consciousness of mankind.

This was vitally important, for growing out of the development of the scientific consciousness and the industrial revolution, there was an increasing trend for man to ignore the realms of spiritual activity and to focus his attentions and energies materially. This was not without positive benefits. Man had been held in bondage by medieval concepts of the spirit and of God which inspired fear and superstition and encouraged ignorance. With the impact of science, man was able to move away from such bondage and into a freedom of mind in which new ideas of great importance could grow. The great political revolutions of the eighteenth and nineteenth centuries reflected his growing attunement to new visions of human rights and freedom and individual dignity, while the growth of research and industry freed him from many of the limitations and fears which had held him in bondage through the centuries. Since many New Age energies are mental in nature, it was necessary for this development of man's knowledge and mind to take place. His consciousness began to expand under the impact of new discoveries, new inventions, new concepts, and he was able to receive more of the energies of growth pouring out to him from the Cosmic Christ and the Solar Logos. As the Earth Logos moved toward the time of his initiation into a new consciousness and life, man was equally propelled along at an accelerating rate.

The disadvantage was that this development was primarily along material lines, which tended to enhance his involvement with the forces and Beings of materialization and form. This created a condition, only a hundred years ago, in which man's mind began to close, for he felt that all important knowledge about the universe had already been gained. Creation was seen as if it were a great clock, a manifestation of purely mechanical laws acting without purpose or guiding intelligence, and man was seen as just a very small cog in this vast universal machine. Any suggestion of unseen spiritual forces or intelligences at work behind the physical appearances was laughed at as being a child's story, a superstition or even madness. The world became increasingly divided between the rationalists, the materialists, the scientists, and the religious, the mystics, the believers in unseen realities, with the latter on the defensive before the onslaught of apparently incontestable "scientific proof" of the fallacy of their beliefs. The possibilities of revealing the existence of an etheric earth born in the midst of consciousness and a new revelation of the Christ presence active within evolution to bring such a birth to pass, and having such a revelation accepted and believed, much less acted upon in a meaningful way, were very small.

Then Einstein developed his famous relationship of $E = Mc^2$, the relationship between energy and matter, and the whole picture changed, especially as that relationship was dramatically demonstrated and confirmed by the explosion of the first atomic bomb. This revelation, plus subsequent research into nuclear energy, introduced to the general consciousness of humanity a concept that had been known for centuries by the mystics and the pioneers into expanded consciousness: nothing is solid; there is no true physical matter. All is energy in motion, and solidity is an illusion produced by the relativity of certain of these motions of vibrations. Further, it was found that on some level all this energy was linked into a unified field or a manifestation of oneness. Along with this realization came the discovery of other dimensions of energy expressing within the atom, such as a fourth dimension in which the electron can apparently function beyond the three dimensions of our physical world: dimensions as real and potent as the material ones, in which the physical atom had roots of some nature. To the occultist, man was beginning to discover, through his exoteric science, the reality of the etheric plane.

Thus, in less than a hundred years, man's world-view underwent a complete reversal from one of rigidity, materialism, close-mindedness and form-orientation to one which may see all creation as the manifestation of an unseen and unified energy field expressing itself as various forms but retaining its essential oneness, a world-view that is open to appreciating, if not fully understanding as yet, the reality of spiritual dimensions of power beyond the physical. Indirectly, through the evolution of nuclear research, man can appreciate a Presence that says "*I am in all things. I am the life from which all form springs. I am the life of all,*" for this description could fit this fundamental universal energy. It is revealed that the root of all material expression is an energy, a spirit, which creates the manifestations of form. A change in the expression of this energy would bring about a change in the form, as demonstrated materially in the experimental transmutation of lead into gold through the use of the cyclotron. It is also demonstrated in life as the changes which occur for a person when he has an inner change of consciousness.

Along with these tremendous revelations in the field of nuclear research came other events to impact upon human consciousness and awaken it to its role in the evolution of Earth. The accelerating rise in population tied with the corresponding rise in pollution and the disruption of the natural ecology bring forcefully to man the necessity for a change in his consciousness if he is to survive on Earth as a physical being. All of these revelations and insights and challenges, fermenting within human consciousness, completed the preparation. Through the centuries the new heaven and the new earth had been forming in the midst of the normal evolutionary flow. The Christ had been building his power, setting into motion the attractive forces that would draw from the world all that would be needed to give reality to this new life. Man's consciousness had been comparably influenced. The time for Revelation was here. The Water Bearer of Aquarius began to pour his new energies out upon the earth. The New Age was here. Now the chalice had to be raised up to receive this outpouring. The false labours were past. The time had come for the birth.

Chapter 14

Revelation!

Like most great events, the birth of the New Age occured quietly, without fanfare, deep within the inner consciousness of Earth. The true event always occurs on levels of causal consciousness, levels of mind and imagination from whence comes that spark of ideation that sets the creative energies of the etheric aflame with complementary formative manifestations. Once the event has been conceived and given life on this high creative level of consciousness, the rest is simply the outworking and reflection of that event within the worlds of time, space and matter.

The time had come. The energies of the New Age were being released. Though Earth was still racked in conflict and suffering, yet the preparations had gone well and now the Earth Logos could reveal the new energy structure, his new etheric body, which could receive these energies in safety. He was ready for his initiation into the new. In describing this, one must necessarily use words which imply physical concepts rather than the pure events of formless spirit. I speak in parable rather than in accurate description. Yet, the process is simple to understand. A change can occur instanteously in consciousness, if there has been a build-up toward it. This change may not be reflected in form at first, but eventually it will be. For the Earth Logos, it was like moving from a used house, in which the wiring was frayed and incomplete and not suitable to receive the new currents flowing in from the cosmic mains, into a new house with new wiring which could receive these energies.

It was a true initiation in which the consciousness of the Earth Logos died to the old and was reborn to the new. His past identity was transmuted into a new one which expressed itself through a new body of purified and radiant energy. It was as if an explosion of Light ripped through the old etheric body, altering its characteristics and raising it into a new level and form already prepared for it, leaving behind only a memory, an etheric "shell," a corpse, a thought-form of what it had been. Yet it was a thought-form with a residue of power, much of which came from the consciousness of mankind. Thus, there became two worlds, one of the old, one of the new. Both had attractive power, the former through the attractiveness of habit and the inertial resistance to change. The new heaven or new etheric, however, had the true power, for it was filled with the expanded life of the christed Earth Logos and it was also receiving the outpouring of fresh and stimulating cosmic energies. The old world, manifesting the reflective etheric, now had no power to grow, only to go on expressing as it always had; the formative etheric became filled with the new power of the Aquarian cycle. There was the Christ fully revealed.

Because of this change in the energies flowing through the etheric, all atomic structure had to undergo a subtle change in order to attune to the formative energies from which it secures its substance and existence. All nuclear energy became transmuted from its attunement to the old etheric "wiring" to that of the new. In this fashion, every atom of matter must either attune to this new life of the Earth Logos and reflect his raised consciousness or, through the law of attraction, it must disappear from the life and awareness of the new and be attracted elsewhere where it would fit in with greater harmony. In essence, the earth must complement its heaven, the physical plane must be attuned to the etheric that gives it sustenance. With a new heaven, a new physical earth had to begin to develop. This development did not take place in terms of new mountains or new valleys; it took place in terms of a new energy, a new Light flowing through the atomic nucleus, a sub-atomic Revelation. This could release from the etheric the Christ life which had entered there at the time of Jesus. This was the true resurrection and ascension, the planetary Second Coming.

Here we see the drama of the past several centuries and especially of the past twenty-five hundred years before us. There are the advanced souls of the race seeking to bridge the gap between the form-oriented consciousness of Earth evolution and the consciousness of the Cosmic Christ. There is the Buddha, rising on the crest of this aspiration, leading the way through the strength of his own dedicated and illumined consciousness to touch and form the first links with the Cosmic Christ. Thus, the way was prepared and the link strengthened until, through the person and consciousness of Jesus and his unfoldment of Christhood, the Cosmic Christ descended and entered the life of Earth on all of its levels.

This was the occult crucifixion, the entry of this cosmic level of life and consciousness into a much lower pattern of energy. Yet, from that level alone could the Cosmic Christ work truly to stimulate and uplift the evolution of Earth life. When the highly potent energies of the Aquarian cycle would radiate upon the world, they would call him forth, like a magnet drawing up iron filings, and he would arise from this imprisonment within matter. He would not arise alone, for through the work on the inner and outer planes over the centuries, Earth life would be attuned enough to him that it would arise with him, which was the point of the whole exercise. The energies of the etheric would lift into a higher field of consciousness and activity where they would be properly and safely receptive to Aquarian energies. The building of the new etheric world was the creation of a mold into which these arising energies could flow and become stabilized as a new heaven and a new earth.

The release of new energies by the Solar Logos signalled the time for the initiation of the Earth Logos. Under the impact of stimulation flowing from solar and cosmic sources, the Earth Logos expanded his consciousness, anchored the new energies within himself on his highest levels and formed the link with the Aquarian cycle. At the same time, the Christ life arose, carrying with it the etheric energies of Earth and linking them with the great thought-form of the new world which had been building over the centuries. At that point, it became a thought-form no more, but the true body of Earth, a body sufficiently pure and vibrant to handle New Age energies, a body of love and truth, and occultly speaking, a resurrection body of the Christ. The old etheric body or matrix of energy-flow was left as a disintegrating "corpse," a thought-form itself, now that the vital energies of growth and creativity and life had been shifted to a higher level and into another energy matrix. This whole process can be described as the resurrection and the ascension, as the Christ becomes the life of a new heaven and a new earth.

Literally, the Christ presence, previously obscured by matter and slow vibrations, is revealed in the new etheric energies. Any consciousness can perceive and commune with him there. His life and energies have been released into a freedom and power of activity without precedence within the affairs of Earth. This is the true coming again of the Christ, for with the death and ascension of Jesus and the entry of the Christ into the densities of Earth, he passed out of the mortal knowledge of man. Men could still find him if they looked deeply within themselves, but for many this was too difficult a task. The Christ, for them, became simply a symbol, a distant god, an image to worship and towards which to aspire. Now, though, he walks amongst us again, though clothed in etheric energy, and his presence quickens the etheric and spiritual life of all who can open in love and peace and, responding, arise to his level. More and more are becoming aware of his life with us; many of these who are becoming attuned in this way seem as messiahs to others and will tend to attract groups about themselves, even identifying themselves as being the Second Coming. Yet, the true Second Coming has occurred and is this revelation and release of Christ life within the inner planes of Earth and affecting the physical planes as well. It is not a person; it is a life which quickens a comparable Christ life within each of us, revealing itself through group activity and a greater love flow within individuals. The Christ is arising within each of us in response to his arising in the macrocosm of our planetary environment. Within each of us is the Second Coming, revealing itself more powerfully as time goes on. Undoubtedly this will make possible the service amongst men of great Beings of Light and evolution, but the Second Coming is a universal experience, not confined to any one person or group of people.

The new revelation of the Christ presence and the vast increase in his ability to influence the affairs of Earth through his having become one with the evolution of Earth is, in itself, an exciting and unparalleled event. It fills the inner realms of consciousness with increasing Light and love and power and makes it easier for human consciousnesses to become one with him, discovering their inner Christ as well. Yet, all this tremendous adventure of several thousand years, though magnificent in itself, is in preparation for a still greater event. The Second Coming and the stimulation of Christ energies within the lives of men and Nature are in preparation for another Revelation. After all, this action of the Christ was to prepare the "wiring," so to speak, to receive a new outflow of current from the "universal mains." Now that preparation is complete; the wiring of the new etheric body of Earth is ready and we receive this new current, the energies of the New Age.

. . . I speak in preparation for a Being whom you have invoked in your desire to embody and to pioneer a new dimension of consciousness for mankind, a Being who is the Regent for energies brought from beyond your system. . . . Where gateways are created, I may enter and where I enter, I prepare the way for One greater than myself who comes to add new energies to earth. . . . He bears with him energies new on earth and stimulating from the earth and all its kingdoms new responses. . . . The Regent of these energies . . . is himself Limitless Love and Light and more beyond. . . .

In this fashion, Limitless Love and Truth spoke of this new outpouring of energies and of the approach and revelation of a great Being of love and Light and "more beyond." What can be greater than the presence of Limitless Love and Truth? What can go beyond the power and glory of the Second Coming? The new life, the new truth, the new Revelation of the Cosmic Christ, for which all this activity has been in preparation, is greater. Having prepared Earth to receive him as a bridegroom, the Cosmic Christ now comes arrayed in his wedding splendour. He comes bearing the gifts of higher awareness for mankind, the sharing in his greater life. The next evolutionary step is greater than the one that preceded it and prepared the way, just as the opportunities and growth of the New Age prepare the way for still greater advances in consciousness to come. We have already spoken of the analogy of the "wiring." The new, increased currents of stimulation flowing in from the higher dimensions give more power and unfoldment to the races of Earth, and the wiring was necessary. Limitless Love and Truth is the personification of the essence of the Christ teachings; it represents the kind of consciousness and life which the Christ taught, the kind of life necessary if a Being is to receive New Age energies. Thus, Limitless Love and Truth are necessary to prepare the way before the Cosmic Christ, in his new appearance, can enter a planetary or a human consciousness and reveal there his new gifts of life, of Truth and of Limitless Love.

This is a New Age, a time of new revelation, new energies, of greater potency than anything previously released on Earth. Yet, that which has been revealed before provides the foundation for this Revelation. Limitless Love and Truth have been seed-ideas within the heart of Earth and of mankind for centuries. Under the impact and stimulus of the Christ, these ideas have been given life and have grown within the womb of consciousness. Once released into the consciousness of the Earth Logos and of mankind, Limitless Love and Truth provide the inspired vision and life of service which can perceive and receive the energies of the Beloved, the Cosmic Christ appearing as the Regent of Aquarian dispensations. Only Love and Truth (acting as balance and sensitive discrimination) can perceive and receive these new energies, which are highly stimulating and constructive. Only Love and Truth can provide the embrace in which the Cosmic Beloved can become one with the planes of Earth, for through Love and Truth these planes have been uplifted to where he can approach them more on his own level of transcendent Light and power. This embrace has occurred. With the creation and activation of the new etheric body of Earth, through the arising and release of the energies of the Christ life represented by the terms "Limitless Love and Truth", the Cosmic Christ has entered the auric field of the planet, bringing with him revelations without precedence, truly inaugurating a New Age of consciousness for Earth and all upon it.

There is another world, the world of man's consciousness. As the Second Coming and the subsequent approach of the Cosmic Christ occurred within the subjective and higher realms of Earth, what has been the complementary unfoldment for mankind? The Earth Logos has met and blended successfully with his evolutionary destiny represented by the Aquarian cycle. Can the same be said for mankind? The New Age is here now and the Christ is functioning within the inner realms of Earth, both in his ascended state from the depths of his past ministry and in his greater state of Aquarian Revelation. How does this affect the world of men, where many have never heard of a New Age and many of those who have are still awaiting its coming in the midst of fire and earthquake and righteous destruction?

The higher realms of Earth, where all true dramas occur to be reflected later into the lower planes of matter, are realms of comparative formlessness, realms of pure energy, Light and consciousness. Names, as humans use them, have no meaning there. Man's consciousness is still form-oriented, even though he begins to understand the nature of those forms to a more spiritual degree. He thinks in terms of separate, objective Beings with names to identify them, and usually not in terms of universal Presences that live within all things and are

144

essentially nameless. He still interprets events and ideas within the references of physical time and space; he thinks of change in terms of forms, rather than in the more important terms of consciousness. He has not yet fully realized his true functioning within infinity and eternity.

Revelation for man, then, had to unfold in terms he could recognize and understand. Once the momentum of Revelation had begun to lift and change the quality of man's life and consciousness, then this understanding and recognition could be expanded until man could meet these forces of Revelation on their own universal terms, beyond the restrictions of form and physical objectivity.

We have spoken of the "false labors" which, in their own way, embodied the forces of Revelation, even if out of timing in some aspects. There have also been true manifestations over the past two centuries of advance, revelations proper to their own day and preparing the way for more to come. We have mentioned some of the scientific and political aspects of this. On the esoteric side, there has been the release of information and concepts held confidential for centuries within select occult groups. This general release to the lay public of the mystery teachings has come through such avenues as the Theosophical Society, the Anthroposophical Society, New Thought movements and others. There has been a greater blending between the cultures and beliefs of East and West. On the religious side, there is a splendid example of revelation in the life and writings of Pierre Teilhard de Chardin. Through many of these sources, the period of the 1960's was revealed as being highly significant, preparing for even greater unfoldments during the 1970's. One of these advance revelators, Sri Aurobindo, an Eastern sage, spoke over thirty years ago of a new force, which he called the "Supramental," impinging on human consciousness, a force that would be fully released into effective power by 1967.

In 1961, a series of phenomena around the world, but centred in Britain, began to manifest. In connection with these was the appearance of a presence who identified himself simply as Limitless Love and Truth. It was announced by this presence that by Christmas Day of 1967, Limitless Love and Truth would be revealed to the universe through the medium of nuclear evolution. Between these years of 1961 and 1967, expectation developed as to the form this revelation would take. Again, man's consciousness tended to interpret this matter in physical objective terms, with the result that many expected some physical manifestation, even one of cataclysmic proportions, by Christmas 1967. When nothing externally significant appeared to happen then, there was considerable disappointment among those who had been physically oriented. Thousands of other individuals around the world, however, did experience a remarkable release of energy upon the earth from higher dimensions. On 31st December 1967, Limitless Love and Truth announced, "My universal revelation, through the medium of nuclear evolution is complete. . . . The whole of nuclear energy is me and my whole power completely under my control. . . . The universal love flow is increasing. All is well."

In this context, the events of 1968 and 1969 are significant, for it seemed that as the decade drew to a close there was an even further acceleration in the impacts to which human consciousness was subjected. The subject of pollution suddenly emerged into popular awareness as never before and people were confronted with the reality of their planetary and ecological responsibilities. Again and again, man was told in increasingly graphic terms of his oneness with the planet, that all life was interrelated, that one form of life could not unheedingly dominate and destroy other forms of life and their natural habitats without endangering all life, including itself. Many scientists placed man on the list of species endangered with extinction and warned that unless he changed his attitude and approach to the living planet on which he dwells from one of exploitation to one of consideration, care, sensitivity to its needs — in short, to an attitude of love and discrimination and wise judgement (truth) — he faced a world-wide ecological breakdown of major proportions.

Here was a threat to rival and even surpass the danger of nuclear war; it brought man to an increasing awareness that he is part of a whole and that he must function in consideration for the total well-being of that whole if he is to survive and grow. Such an awareness is surely the essence of Limitless Love and Truth. At the same time, as if to emphasize dramatically this idea of the oneness and interdependence of this living planet, man for the first time circled and landed upon a dead world, the moon. Here was a total contrast between the lifeless moon and the living Earth. Photographs of Earth from far out in space were shared around the world, bringing home still further to human conscious and subconscious levels that this is one world, to be handled with care, love and wisdom if it is not to become as lifeless as the moon.

These events and the new awareness and responsibility to the world which they are inspiring confirm the words of Limitless Love and Truth that the "universal love flow is increasing." Since 1967 alone, mankind has become more aware than ever of the need for such a universal and limitless love to be expressed if he is to survive and build a human civilization. This awareness is stimulating groups and people around the world to seek to understand and apply the principles of such a love flow in their lives as never before. It may manifest itself simply as an increased awareness of the community of life of which one is a part and of one's dependence on the well-being of that ecological community, but that is a significant step for a creature that has been notorious throughout history for his self-sufficiency and ignorance of the Whole.

Though we may see that the idea and pattern of Limitless Love and Truth are impressing themselves more strongly and urgently on human awareness, this still leaves some questions. Who — or what — is Limitless Love and Truth and how does this presence and Its appearance to human awareness, in the form of a Being, tie in with the initiation of the Earth Logos, the change of the etheric energies and the birth of a New Age described earlier?

147

I have stated that human consciousness, being form-oriented, requires a revelation that it can recognize in terms of form. Hence, Limitless Love and Truth appeared, not as a formless universal principal (though that is what it essentially is), but as a form, a Being, which humans could recognize and to which they could relate. Often, in different parts of the world, this form was accompanied by some kind of phenomenon designed to attract attention. Man generally loves a show, the more spectacular the better, and the higher levels of being are not above putting on such a show if necessary, though such phenomena are not part of Revelation itself.

This form identified itself as Limitless Love and Truth. These are the essential characteristics, as we have seen, of the energies creating the new etheric body of Earth. They are the qualities needed to be expressed by a consciousness, whether of the planet or of an individual, before the full gift of New Age transformation can be accepted or realized. This form, then, represents the objectification into human awareness of the nature and the direction of the change of consciousness which has occurred on the inner levels to permit reception of New Age energies. It represents the personification of the initiated consciousness of the Earth Logos, releasing his new energies and life through his new etheric body. It also represents the type of consciousness man needs to adopt and express if he is to undergo a comparable initiation.

By Christmas 1967, the initiation of the Earth was complete. The transfusion of energies from the old etheric to the new one had been sufficiently completed; cosmic blessings had been placed upon Earth. The Christ, imprisoned in the tomb of matter for nearly two thousand years, had ascended and blended with the Cosmic Christ approaching with new energies. The New Age had been born. Millions about the world felt this take place as new Light and power flowed into Earth. Those whose minds and hearts were open through anticipation received these energies into themselves with effects still being felt. Many, however, through disappointment, closed their minds, cutting themselves off from direct reception of this increased flow of love and Light, at least for that time.

The next two years were filled with accelerated change and drama as the worlds of man and Nature sought to absorb and to respond to these initial energies of change and evolution. The world sought to stabilize itself in order to prepare for the next outpouring. The New Age, the new heaven and the new earth now existing within the formative etheric, sought to externalize themselves, unfolding in the midst of man's activity, as pioneering individuals attuned to the reality of this new presence and worked to aid its manifestation. The momentum was being established for the blending with the consciousness of the Aquarian Christ and his new energies. By 1970, the time was right for these true New Age energies to begin to descend. Revelation was on the move!

Chapter 15

Limitless Love and Truth

Am I God? Am I a Christ? Am I a Being come to you from the dwelling places of the infinite? I am all these things, yet more. I am Revelation. (I am) that Presence which has been before the foundations of the Earth. . . . The Earth . . . is my body. I am the life from which all form springs. I am the Womb and all must enter through me. I am not a Being. I contain all Beings. I am now the life of a new heaven and a new earth. Others must draw upon me and unite with me to build its forms. I am acting within the entire vibrational structure of this planet on all of its levels. I unfold from within it what it has always stored there and which shall form the new.

These are the ways in which Limitless Love and Truth describes itself. It helps if we realize that this is not a Being, as it has stated it is not, but is rather the personification of a state of being now existing and manifesting within the newly initiated and expanded consciousness of Earth life. There are many separate Beings and energies and presences that contribute to this overall state of being. Thus, Limitless Love and Truth is, in a fashion, spokesman for several sources of life and power and energy and speaks from several viewpoints, which can be confusing until we realize that all is one life, one being, anyway. It is one love and one truth approached from several different angles for better communication and understanding.

For example, God is the universal source and life. There is not one place, one thing, one time that does not include his presence. God is the life within all things. He contains all things. Limitless Love and Truth are certainly essential characteristics of the Divine. As the Earth Logos and all Beings who share his life realize a further unfoldment of their indwelling Divinity, they are able to unite more intimately and effectively with the Divinity operative throughout the universe, bringing about a universal revelation. The form of Limitless Love and Truth may thus speak to human consciousness as the personification of this new state of planetary consciousness and universal linking, a state of increased awareness of the presence of Divinity. This is the voice of God, for God is the essential voice of all things.

Secondly, Limitless Love and Truth speaks with the voice of the Earth Logos whose new etheric life is the source of energy for all physical manifestation, the "womb" through which all must pass to enter into form expression. It proclaims the power and radiance of a new heaven and a new earth vibrating within the consciousness of Earth and calls men to attune to that reality and to express it.

Thirdly, Limitless Love and Truth speaks with the voice of the Christ. This is the universal educative presence, calling forth from within life and form "what it has always stored there and which shall form the new." This presence always stimulates the continual emergence of progressively newer and greater manifestations of Divinity from the storehouse of potential within consciousness. The Christ, as Limitless Love and Truth, calls out of man that love, that Light, that wisdom and truth which will enable him to build the new world within himself and in his environment. This dispensation, this educational stimulus, is represented by its source, the Cosmic Christ. Limitless Love and Truth are certainly his qualities as he comes to give Earth new energies, new teachings, new unfoldments, new revelations, new visions, new understanding and new life commensurate with the expanded consciousness of the Earth Logos. Regent of Aquarian energies, he and his helpers come to this world from the Solar Logos and the stars beyond to inaugurate a new order.

Limitless Love and Truth also represents another aspect of the Christ, the saviour aspect which, incarnating into matter, counteracted the downward pull of the materializing forces by providing a strong stimulation to the arising, evolutionary urge of spirit and life. The arising and release of this Christ life from its imprisonment into the freedom of activity upon the new etheric is the essence of the Second Coming. From that level, it can work to stimulate a similar arising and release into the awareness of individual man of his indwelling Christ Spirit. This, for each individual, is the true coming again of the Christ and provides the foundation of consciousness to receive the New Age outpourings. Limitless Love and Truth does reveal this Second Coming and personifies the presence of the Risen Christ seeking to make his reality known to mankind.

I am all these things, yet more. It is imaginable that there is a force that is more than a Christ, more than a Being from the infinite, but what is more than God? This statement of Limitless Love and Truth can cause confusion until we realize that this form is something of a teaching aid created to personify certain universal and (by physical standards) formless qualities and intelligences. As such, it seeks to meet man on a form-oriented level which he can comprehend, yet at the same time prepare him to move into a freer, more abstract consciousness.

God, Christ, Beings — all these are terms which have ancient meanings to man. They have collected around themselves innumerable thought-forms, as different cultures, races and individuals have defined what these terms mean. How many religious wars have been fought between cultures which believed they were worshipping different gods? How many Christian sects have been separated because of different definitions of what God is and of who and what Christ was? What Limitless Love and Truth seeks to express here is that he represents the qualities we normally associate with God, and with Christ, but he also represents the true qualities of both, which are beyond words. He is saying, in essence, "I am all these recognizable thought-forms which you have formed of God and of Christ and of great Beings, but I am also more. I am aspects of Divinity, of God, which you

152

have not yet learned to recognize but which will be revealed to you in this New Age."

We can say that Limitless Love and Truth is really Christ, or God, or a Master from an exalted plane of being, but in doing this, we only place him into categories which are familiar to us, which have been built up through the past. We miss the implications of his being a *new* revelation, a Revelation seeking to expand our consciousness beyond the thinking and imaging of the past and into a new awareness. "I am more than you have learned to conceive of," is what he is implying to us, and he calls us to expand our consciousnesses beyond the customary and traditional concepts. The full knowledge of what Limitless Love and Truth is awaits the man who can enter the higher levels of his own heart and mind through actually living a life based on these qualities. Each of us is the presence of Limitless Love and Truth. As we learn to accept this and to apply this acceptance in daily life, we shall learn what the great formless, nameless realities behind our images are. We shall know God as our Father, our Beloved, our Self and more beyond which cannot be verbalized, only experienced. Furthermore, by freeing Limitless Love and Truth from certain stereotyed forms and images, we are better able to recognize the reality of this presence wherever it may be functioning. Far from limiting it to our particular sect or creed or group or nationality or teaching, we can see and appreciate its Revelation wherever and within whomsoever it manifests, however different this may be in form from what our own training or inclinations would expect. We will be sensitive to the vibrations of love and truth and will be able to go beyond the form in which these qualities are expressing. We learn, by freeing Limitless Love and Truth into its universal nature, that Revelation is not confined to one source, one center, one person or one form but indeed is a world-wide operation affecting all mankind in countless and varied ways which yet have the one similarity of working to uplift and free him into the opportunities of this New Age.

Thus, Limitless Love and Truth is Revelation itself. It is a manifestation designed to stimulate man's mind into new directions of thought and action which will reveal the presence of the New Age to him. It is a gateway to a greater world beyond the present restricted and fear-ridden thinking of present humanity. It is a vision of change through which mankind can pass from its present state of consciousness to a new one, a new heaven from which will flow the inspiration to build a new earth and a new civilization.

One looking upon the world today might feel this an impossible task, but such a one does not take into account the tremendous preparation, over the past several centuries, for this time, not just on planetary levels but within individuals as well. All people have a Divine spirit which will respond to what Limitless Love and Truth represents, but many people have more than that. Over the centuries of exposure to the principles of spiritual life, they have built up within themselves an inner structure of consciousness analogous to the new etheric body of Earth. Though unexpressed, it has nonetheless been building. It is a New Age body, awaiting stimulation to call it forth, awaiting a spark to set it aflame with revealed power and Light, transforming the life of the individual. With the seemingly insurmountable challenges besetting modern man, he is realizing his insufficiency; he is being shocked out of a complacent attitude. He is turning within for help, for answers. He is exposing his inner spiritual core to receive the spark that will alight it.

Throughout the world, no matter what form it takes, what words it uses, true Revelation is the energy that gives that spark. It has already set the inner planes aflame with new life. It can and will do the same for any individual who opens himself to the transforming and regenerating energies now moving through this world. Limitless Love and Truth is a manifestation of Revelation, of these catalytic energies, the very personification of the new. As individuals respond, they will find themselves literally moving into a new world of consciousness from which they can act as potent forces to reform the outer conditions of their world. Revelation is the call to the new, to high adventure in creativity; it is a vision, a hope, a promise, a reality. Man may fight and resist the new initially, but he has never successfully halted its advance, for it is in his very nature to grow and to change and to explore new realms. This is what Revelation asks him to do now. It calls directly to the New Age body slumbering within him, and this body will respond.

Limitless Love and Truth is the essence and personification of Revelation. It is the living vision of the new. At this time in human affairs, there is no more potent force.

Chapter 16

Two Worlds

I move steadily towards the consummation of my Revelation. For I attract to me now Lovers from beyond the stars to unite with me and pour their seed into Earth and transform it. I invoke and invite from beyond Beings who come to impregnate me with powers and energies from what I am beyond this system. (These Beings and I) form the body of a new heaven and . . . a new earth. (I draw) to me the elements that will form the new heaven and the new earth and this motion proceeds . . . towards its perfect revelation. Your world shall become . . . two worlds. I am the body of one; I am the shepherd of the other. There are two worlds: one of the old, one of the new. Heed not the voices that speak to the old but know that I am within you, for I would proclaim to you what comes from beyond. I would have you unite with it and be impregnated with it as I am within you and receive from my greater being beyond this planet.

New energies, new life, new civilization, two worlds, old and new, separating until they *"perceive each other no more"* — surely these are proper elements for a cosmic drama. One might almost be tempted to speak in terms of a day of judgment, a time of separating the chaff from the wheat, were it not for other statements of Revelation: *"I am in both (worlds). Not one atom of life stands beyond me. Shall I forsake those who even now drift apart into a destiny of their own . . .? I am their shephered as well. I am with you and I am with them. Not one man, not one creature goes apart from me. Whatever befalls the old world, I am there. I have not come to sift the good from the bad. I am not a judge. I simly am what I am. If you are what I am, then you are of me. None are saved. None are lost."*

These are provocative statements as well. What is the nature of this separation of the two worlds? How will it occur, especially in view of yet another statement of Limitless Love and Truth: *"If you would build the new as I call upon you to do, then you cannot set yourselves against the old. There can be no separation."*?

To clarify this, we must first understand how these two worlds were created and what is their nature. We have already discussed how, with the translation of etheric energies to a higher level, the thought-pattern of the old etheric was left behind as something analogous to a corpse or a memory. This is certainly the creation of two worlds, and we will discuss this aspect of it more fully later. At this point, something needs to be said about the reason behind this separation. Here a little story may help.

There were once two brothers who had been blessed with the riches of life. Handsome and charming, they were also very wealthy. It was often their custom to take journeys by foot through the country and, in spite of their wealth, they travelled very simply. On one such journey, they stayed at the home of a poor farmer. Though he only had enough land to support himself and his family, he still considered himself very fortunate, for he had two beautiful daughters. Needless to say, the two brothers fell in love with them.

In talking privately between themselves, the brothers decided not to reveal their true estate to the daughters, for they wished the girls to love them for themselves and not because they were wealthy. Thus, they courted the girls as if they were only poor country folk like the farmer and his family.

Soon, this plan began to work for the first brother, for the heart of the elder daughter responded to him and filled with love. The other brother was not so fortunate, for though the younger daughter was attracted to him, she was unhappy with her poor estate. Her mind was filled with thoughts of future wealth and position, visions which seemed to hold little hope of fulfilment in the person of a handsome but poor wanderer.

In time, the elder brother and his beloved realized that there was no longer need for courting. Their love was strong and sure. The time for marriage had arrived, no purpose being served by further waiting. The brother knew that the love for him in the girl's heart was so developed that the revelation of the wealth which would be hers would only add to the blessing of their relationship. The younger brother was glad for his kinsman's good fortune, yet he still hoped to win the heart of the younger daughter away from her thoughts of wealth and power and turn it to love. So, he asked his brother not to reveal their true fortune but to take his bride away back to their home and there make the truth known to her. In this way, no one would know that he, too, was wealthy. To this the elder brother agreed. After the wedding, he and his bride left the farmer's house and travelled to his home, leaving the younger brother behind to continue wooing the other daughter.

Because this is a love story, we shall give it a happy ending. From time to time, the married couple would visit the home of the farmer. Keeping to the plan, they always went simply, without revealing their wealth, yet they could not hide their joy in the love they shared. Finally, the younger sister began to awaken to this joy and to see the remaining brother in a new light. Perhaps, after all, he could give her something that was far more precious than gold, for was not her sister enjoying a new radiance of happiness? With this change in attitude, the girl began to feel a love growing in her, too. In time, this love grew to where it cast out all other thoughts but those of her beloved and all knew that the time had come when another wedding would be celebrated. Through the strength of her love, the younger sister could now receive the riches which she had once desired and which could have been hers all along had she only learned to open her vision to love.

Within the presence and consciousness of the Christ, whether indwelling within mankind or whether in his transcendent cosmic aspects, there are stored vast riches of crative energies and powers, fabulous treasures of the expanded consciousness. These are energies which enhance the creative and dynamic power of the being, giving greater power and impact to the products of that being's consciousness. If the quality of creativity which that being manifests is dominated by love and an attunement to the well-being of the Whole, as well as a creative discrimination, then he may receive these riches abundantly. If he is yet enmeshed in attachment to form and personality patterns to the exclusion of the higher nature, then he cannot receive these energies. To give them to a consciousness deeply involved with self and separation and materialism would be to intensify the impact of these involvements within the soul, with detrimental effect on that being, just as giving unlimited wealth to an undisciplined individual is to invite him to dissipate himself that much more completely.

Therefore, the Christ did not come to Earth initially in all his spendour. He came in a simpler form, if such a phrase may be used to describe this universal presence! He came concentrating on the aspect of love and he courted the consciousness of mankind, seeking to inspire a presence of love there. In many he succeeded, until the time came when a true wedding could occur and a new relationship develop. He could reveal himself as the Beloved, come to unite with men's consciousnesses and give birth to whole new worlds of creative power and opportunity. The time could not be delayed, and on the higher levels of Earth and within the souls of many men and women this wedding did occur. The New Age was born.

Yet, many people did not awaken fully to this love. They could appreciate its value for others, but their hearts and minds were occupied with other things. After centuries of teaching and demonstration, their consciousnesses dwelt still upon visions of material power and forms. Yet, their presence in the world-soul cannot delay the wedding of those who are ready. The Earth Logos himself has undergone the wedding initiation. Those who can open to and begin expressing a universal love flow find themselves moving into a new world, the world of the Beloved, the Cosmic Christ who, revealing his own greater splendor, can call forth the complementary splendor from with the human soul and consciousness.

What of those who cannot have such riches of inner power unfolded for them lest, in giving them more than their consciousnesses can safely bear, it jeopardizes them? Like the second daughter, they are also loved. Though the Cosmic Christ, in his Aquarian Revelation, moves on to a new world of consciousness with those who can journey with him, he also remains to continue courting those who have yet to respond to the presence of love and truth within themselves. In time, they will awaken also; their wedding will be celebrated and the riches of expanded consciousness become theirs.

It must be seen, therefore, that this division of consciousness is not an act of heavenly judgment. It reflects the presence of two distinct energy-flows affecting consciousness. One is highly potent and uplifting and bears the consciousness upward into expanded potential and power and joy; it is highly constructive and can only truly be sensed and attuned to by a consciousness that is seeking to build, not to destroy. The other energy-flow represents the displaced energies of the old etheric pattern and the motion of the materializing forces. These flow off to a dimension, a place — who can say where — in which they will find balance and harmony again. They have no place in the new world. With which stream a particular individual consciousness moves is decided entirely by his own choice and attunement, by the kinds of energies he is releasing into his world. Are they energies of love, of seeking understanding, of respect, of service, of building, of peace, or are they energies of separation, fear, antagonism, violence, destruction, conflict? Limitless Love and Truth speaks of this personal choice: *"Let men not speculate to which world they belong. Their life . . . their actions decide this. What are they creating as they move amongst me, as I am within all things, within humans, within Nature, within all that is? Who is to decide mentally what is of me [in the new] and what is not? I want no man mentally to judge. . . . First, I must live within you. You must express what I am without limit and then all is revealed perfectly."* Here we see clearly that the dividing factor is not external judgment but internal attitudes as expressed through external actions.

Love unites; it embraces all. It is not divided. It is truth that separates, for truth is that awareness which knows what is right and appropriate to be expressed in the moment and what is not. It is akin to artistic discrimination. It acts to place each person or thing in its proper place where it can receive that universal outflow most beneficial and appropriate to its needs. This is, in essence, an act of love, for nothing is more essentially separating and divisive than being out of place or out of timing, unable fully to connect with what is happening. Truth moves things where they belong according to their expression in the moment. It is the manifestation of the law of attraction. In this instance, certain consciousnesses upon the earth are ready to receive new energies and opportunities; these energies are now available. To prevent them from linking together would be inappropriate, an evil action. Likewise, certain other consciousnesses upon Earth are not ready to receive these energies; they are not opening to them. To make them receive them is also inappropriate for their highest good. So, the two are separated, the first to go to a state of being where the New Age energies are dominant, the second to go where the patterns of the old still hold sway. *"All now move swiftly toward their appointed destinies as their consciousnesses have chosen."* This is the action of truth. Yet, *"not one man, not one creature goes apart from me."* This is the action of a Limitless Love which sees all men and Beings in their true estate of essential Divinity and splendor and knows the oneness of all, which that vision reveals, no matter what the external patterns through which they are expressing may suggest.

We have been talking about two worlds and their separation. What is meant here? Are we to envisage some cataclysmic splitting of Earth, with a new planet physically spinning off from the old one? Not at all. All physical form proceeds from the consciousness that has created it and in

161

which it is rooted. Just as rebirth is fundamentally a process of consciousness, so is this separation of the two worlds, though it will eventually have a physical reflection, as we shall see. We have an example of this in the so-called generation gap. Increasingly, the world of the young is differing from the world of the parents. This is a separation of consciousness. As the older generation passes out of physical expression, the young come more into control of the sources and means of power, such as political, scientific and economic power. Their visions and ideas have increasing dominion upon Earth and with the growth in their ability to implement these ideas, the physical world will change. Certain architectural styles and clothing styles and educational styles will be replaced by others. This is an example of a change in consciousness gradually externalizing itself into a change in physical form expressions.

The gap between the two worlds of Revelation, however, is not between generations. It is between attitudes toward life in its wholeness. On the one hand are those who live in the consciousness of the oneness of life and work to build and serve the best interests of the whole. On the other are those who see only their own interests and exploit the whole to satisfy their personal patterns. This division cuts across generational lines. Many young people today are outwardly sympathetic to the whole but are actually expressing attitudes of selfishness and inconsideration, while many older people are truly expressing the qualities of Limitless Love and Truth. This division between the two worlds cannot be drawn between cultures, between races, between age groups. It cannot be determined mentally. It is determined, as we have seen, by an inner orientation. Some seek to escape, to destroy, to strike out. They are of the old. Others seek to build, to change through a positive vision, to heal, to bless. They are of the new.

Understanding the factors of consciousness that are causing this separation is most important, for it gives us a practical vision of what we need to be and to do in order to fulfil the promise of Revelation within our own lives. Yet, we still have the question of the mechanics of this change. What are these two worlds? What will happen to those who cannot attune to the new? Where will they go? Here we can only suggest answers, for the true answers lie beyond verbalization, as they deal with patterns of consciousness and levels of energy dimensions which we have not fully begun to understand in our culture. Furthermore, it is not really important to know where the old pattern will go; we are assured that it is shephereded by the Christ and will be fully ministered to by this cosmic presence. It is most important for us to concentrate on the visions of the new and to externalize them through constructive and appropriate action.

However, there are a few words which can be said about where the old world and those attuned to it will go. Throughout creation there are infinite spheres of environment representing and educating all stages of consciousness development. Some of these are physical planets, like Earth; others exist on higher dimensional levels. It is possible that many from Earth will find themselves attracted to such other spheres or planets within the universe which are at a stage of growth comparable to what Earth has moved out of.

There is another pattern, though, which is more likely. Earth is really like a vast mansion with the ground floor representing the physical plane. Only a small percentage of the souls associated with Earth evolution are ever on the physical at once; they tend to travel together like groups, like classes in university which move together as a wave through the various levels and all graduate together. As Earth moves through cycles, certain kinds of souls are attracted to the ground floor and the others work and learn on higher levels. When the cycle ends, the one life-wave moves into higher levels and is replaced by another. In other words, some live part of the time upstairs and part of the time on the ground floor.

With the transference of life energy from the thought-form of the old world to the thought-form of the new one, the old world now exists only as a disintegrating world memory. Those who stand upon it for support find that it is becoming like shifting sand, unstable, confusing, filled with stress. Yet, they cannot reach up and out in consciousness to attain and stand on the rock of the new world. It would not be without precedence for them to be withdrawn into the inner worlds, to live in an "upstairs" room which would reflect the needs of their consciousnesses and minister to those needs. In other words, the planet or plane or level to which they will go, through the law of attraction, may not be "somewhere else". It may be another level of Earth's own consciousness where they can be contained and ministered to until such time as they can be released safely into physical embodiment again. There is a suggestion of this in the Bible where it speaks of Satan and his minions (the materializing forces and those who attune to them too exclusively) being bound for a thousand years and then released again. Thus, these ones could be withdrawn into an inner realm that would be their home while the consciousnesses attuned to the New Age were active in building the new world physically and psychically. Then, when these new energies were sufficiently stabilized, these ones could be released back into physical embodiment to complete their transformation into a more spiritual pattern, to celebrate their own wedding feast, as it were.

Whether this is indeed the pattern or whether these ones shall be moved entirely out of the Earth pattern (which is least probable except for certain individual cases), the main point is that they will lose, for the time being, their access to the etheric planes of power and the ability to control or influence the developments upon Earth. Perhaps they will be in a place to observe and benefit from these developments (which is quite likely) but will have no power to interfere. They will have moved from an active state to a relatively passive one. They will be shielded from the increased creative powers flowing through the formative etheric to which New Age individuals will be able to attune quite readily. Yet, through observation, they will learn of the love and joy and truth needed to wield these powers safely. When they again gain access to the planes of creative energy, they will know better how to express themselves. The two worlds, having been separated, will come together again and truth will manifest the unity of love, just as the two sisters were reunited through their love for the brothers, though the younger sister had to wait longer for this joy and unity.

We have already spoken of two worlds that have always existed, one rooted in the creative consciousness of the Earth Logos, the other expressing the developing creativeness of man's consciousness. The first world gives us the basic physical world with all its kingdoms of Nature. It is the source for all life, including man's, for he derives his nourishment from the earth. The second world represents the creations of man plus the changes he had made in the physical earth through his actions upon Nature.

The first world has always been beautiful, filled with a Light and a power that all too few humans have paused to see or to consider. With the initiation of the Earth Logos, the radiance seeking to express through this world has increased. All Nature must expand and adapt to manifest this greater energy. This is already occurring. This may not create a different physical configuration for the new world; it requires no great cataclysmic activity to manifest this greater life and Light. In areas where man's world has impinged destructively upon the natural one, creating pollution or ecological imbalance, there may be cleansing manifestations of some power, but the New Age does not require destruction to announce its arrival and may indeed be masked by such outer phenomena. The energies it brings are purely creative and constructive; to concentrate on destruction through expectation or desire is only to align one's consciousness with the vibrations of the old.

The patterns of Nature have always been God-attuned and beautiful. It is only man's consciousness that has seen it otherwise. Hence, it is not the physical world of Nature that needs so much to change in order to manifest the new life.

Undoubtedly there will be some changes and mutations as required, but this can be done without undue stress, for the forms of Nature, through the contact of the Devic and Elemental worlds, are already attuned and pure.

It is in the second world, the world of man's consciousness, that the true cataclysms may be felt. Man creates that he may possess his creations. He is loath to give up his possessions in order to allow for change and new crativity. Hence, man's creations tend to crystallize and become dogmatic forms existing long past their time of usefulness. Neither truth nor Love are fulfilled by this. Thus, the first impact of Aquarius was the introduction of interim energies designed to shatter the outdated thought-forms and creations and to free the imprisoned consciousnesses that they might catch a newer and more uplifting vision. Such energies may express destructively, and we witness the greatest cataclysms now occurring within the cultures and institutions and traditions of man. Yet, though important, such energies are only interim and do not represent the qualities of the New Age. They represent the pattern of truth as it removes what is no longer appropriate, what is out of place or out of timing.

The true energies of the New Age represent another aspect of truth which recognizes and encourages that which is in timing and in place, that which is right and appropriate. New Age energies, brought to man and to Earth by the Cosmic Christ and his helpers, the "Lovers from beyond the stars," are attuned only to the images and visions which the New Age will express. They are constructive, energizing, nourishing; they enhance the manifestation of these images and visions. They are not destructively in conflict with the old, because for them the old simply does not exist. It is a corpse, a memory, a racial thought-form in the process of disintegration. Other energies are assisting this process of disintegration, but New Age energies deal with the reality which the New Age represents, not with memories that are essentially unreal and which have no future. Nor can they deal with consciousnesses which express in destruction or rebellion against the old, for such consciousnesses are still reflecting the qualities of the old. The highest form of protest is to build the new, not to fight the old; all who seek this form of constructive protest, who build the new and give it life, will find themselves increasingly attuned to these energies and being strengthened, supported and empowered by them. They will increasingly live in the household of the Beloved, there to receive the treasures of that union with the universal Christ.

The two worlds do not have to separate cataclysmically even in human consciousness. The old world may well disappear with a whimper rather than a bang. We can already see a suggestion of how this can work. Those who live in harmony with the principles of constructive creation, of love and of truth, and are strengthened by the nourishing energies of the New Age, experience a greater sense of inner peace and calm than those who are not attuned to these forces. They are open, in trust and faith, to the higher consciousness that they may be inspired. Those who are responsive to and expressing energies of destruction, fear, hatred and separation do not have these higher sources to draw upon; they are supported only by their own energies of disintegration, which lead to self-disintegration.

As the New Age increases its manifestation, changes are coming at an accelerating rate; mass media broadcast the crises of the world daily into the homes of millions of people, emphasizing in graphic terms the tension and fear and conflict which change can produce. Fear and worry are man's constant companions, pulling at him psychically and physically, sapping his energy and building up his inner stresses. These are forces, destructive patterns of thought and feeling, which exact a heavy toll on the balance of the physical body. They tend to disintegrate the wholeness of the being on which health depends. The person who attunes to the whole of life, through his love and wisdom, maintains his own integrity, his own wholeness. He is strengthened, upheld in the face of these pressures and turmoils. His consciousness does not share in thoughts and feelings of destruction, fear, violence or hatred and therefore he does not create these conditions within himself. He is creating the new, so the energies of the new support him. He cannot be sapped by the disintegration of the old world.

This is not true for the individual whose consciousness is still creating the mental and emotional conditions that characterize the old world. Blaming his environment for all that happens to him, instead of realizing that his own consciousness is the creative source for all that is attracted into his personal world, he is in conflict with the whole. Thus, he does not experience Wholeness outside of himself nor within himself. He has no protection against the destructive, disintegrating powers generated in the world. He has no inner rock of strength or of peace on which to stand. He is open to tension, to stress, to loss of energy. He is like a clock which can only run down, for he is not in touch with the hand that can wind him up.

Such a person is susceptible to "stress diseases" such as heart attack, nervous breakdowns, strokes and so forth. His body loses its inner resiliancy, its power to rebuild itself. Already more people are dying of these stress diseases than ever before as people's bodies begin literally to disintegrate under the impact of the increasing stress of modern society and rapid change.

There is a simple difference between a person who is inwardly at peace and attuned to a source of strength and power greater than human level problems and one who is attuned to conflict with such problems and consequently to a consciousness of fear and anxiety and limitation. it is also known that people who are undergoing inner emotional stress are more accident prone, another consequence of this simple difference. Yet, it is just this simple difference that may be the key to the separation of the two worlds, not through something exotic, such as a miraculous translation of an elect few into some other plane, but through something as prosaic as people dying in significantly increasing numbers because they cannot live at peace within themselves and with their world nor can they create conditions of harmony. Earth itself, as a physical place, does not need to be cataclysmically altered in order to usher in the New Age. The two worlds do not need to separate within Nature, where most patterns are already properly balanced and attuned. It is in man's consciousness that this separation between the forces of building and the forces of self-perpetuating conflict needs to take place, and it may well occur through the personal disintegration of millions of personal worlds because the consciousnesses creating those worlds were unable to express a unifying life of love, truth and wisdom.

Still, there is another pattern which is also a key to this separation. We have discussed the disintegrating energies active within the old world of consciousness as agents of separation. The building energies within the new world of consciousness are also emphasizing this contrast and separation between the two worlds. An understanding of the arising earth is as important as an understanding of the disintegrating one, more important really, for it is the world that now calls for our allegiance. Here we are given an insight in the words of Limitless Love and Truth: *"I have not come to sift the good from the bad. I am not a judge. I simply am what I am. If you are what I am, then you are of me. None are saved. None are lost. If you would build the new as I call upon you to do, then you cannot set yourselves against the old. There can be no separation."*

In spite of what appears at first, this is not a contradiction but an expression of the nature of the energies of building and new creativity. These are not energies of separation nor of conflict. They are energies flowing into the molds, the basic thought-forms, images and ideas of the new heaven and the new earth, in order to give those patterns reality of expression on all levels, including the physical. For these energies and the Beings who represent and channel them from cosmic levels, the old patterns have no reality, no existence. How, then, can they conflict with something that is only a phantom? Man may see a conflict becuase his consciousness still thinks in those terms; thinking that way, he could use these new energies in conflict with the old. This is quite contrary to their nature. They will not flow through such a consciousness.

For this reason, Revelation asks us not to judge, in the sense of creating a situation of conflict, nor to set ourselves against the old. Because there is no separation in the consciousness of the new world, there can be no separation in our consciousness if we would be at one with that world. Our consciousness must reflect and manifest the qualities which are of the new. To know the new, one must *be* the new. To engage in conflict with the disintegrating patterns is to be at one with them, just as to use violence to stop violence is to defeat one's essential purpose. The old will separate itself naturally, as we have seen; it need not be a task we take onto ourselves. Limitless Love and Truth has stated that no Being goes anywhere without his being with him; all are enfolded in his love and presence. We are asked to manifest that same consciousness. If so, then obviously we cannot speak of those who are "saved" and those who are "lost". If separativeness is one of the characteristics of the old world, then it has place in any consciousness that would manifest the new world.

Truth reveals to us the patterns of the new and inspires us where to direct our energies in new Creation. Our energies are needed in building, in revealing in our own lives and actions and creations the qualities of the new world, new vision, new adventure and new life-styles. In dealing with a bad habit, one should not concentrate on the habit. One concentrates on the new pattern one wishes to manifest and directs one's attention and powers to it. As it becomes strengthened into manifestation, it displaces the old pattern which simply disappears. So it is with the separation of the two worlds. Something must replace the world that is disintegrating, and something has replaced it. It exists on the etheric and is even now bursting into form and recognition around the world. Yet, it requires that all who would be its sons and daughters must give their energies to opening themselves to this new earth aborning and concentrate on building it. As the new heaven and the new earth come into increasingly stronger and more stable manifestation, they will naturally displace the old world while providing a new pattern to which people can attune.

Because the energies flowing in the old world and its heaven or source-consciousness are disintegrative, forms which reflect these energies have no growing or sustaining power. Individuals who attune to the old will find themselves unable to be truly creative; what they build will not last. On the other hand, New Age individuals are attuned to the highly creative and magnetic energies which characterize this Aquarian cycle. What they put their hands to will prosper; what they build will last; what they create will grow. Thus, the objective world will increasingly take on New Age aspects and forms because only these forms will have the life and power and attunement to survive and prosper and develop.

In this way, the two worlds are separating, one fading out, the other becoming clearer, stronger, more powerful in its expression. The contrast between the two is manifested daily and will become more distinct. As more energies of consciousness and support are put into the development of the new, the more smoothly, the more swiftly, the less chaotically this separation will occur. As the new patterns become known through revelation and demonstration, they lose their mystery; hence, they are not regarded by men through fear of the unknown. Furthermore, many of the patterns of the new world carry on to higher levels the patterns and traditions of the past, for the old world referred to here is not necessarily the world of the past but one of attitudes and ideas, a world of consciousness and the energies it generates. The past of mankind is the seed out of which the future emerges. Much of the wisdom, development, beauty and joy of man's heritage will be brought forward as essential parts of the New Age. This is another reason why one cannot set oneself against the old world lest, in the heat of conflict, one throws out needful patterns from the past. By concentrating on building the new, the proper tools and materials are drawn out of man's heritage and used appropriately. Everything else that has served its purpose and must now disappear will do so naturally.

This, then, is the cosmic context of Revelation. It is a drama of consciousness and the development of consciousness. It is a story of cycles, with each cycle bringing into action new energies, new opportunities and new challenges for life and requiring appropriate change. All that can change moves on into the new cycle perfectly. All that cannot is placed into a "remedial" realm where it is either brought back into balance with the advancing life or is directed elsewhere through the law of attraction.

We are in a time of turmoil because these two worlds are separating. Man is faced with choices and challenges that must be met if he is to survive. In the past, man has been able to avoid this confrontation by running away from it. Rather than learning to settle differences between himself and others, rather than learning to love and work in cooperation with his neighbor, he has moved; he has migrated to where he could build his own personal world. When he has failed to understand and cooperate with Nature and has desolated the land, he has moved again.

Now, he can no longer run. There are no more virgin territories to settle. People are everywhere and mass media bring our neighbours throughout the world right into our living rooms. The world is shrinking and so are its natural resources. When man destroys his land or his water, he cannot ride off into the sunset to find more. This time he dies of starvation or thirst, or he learns to share with others, to give and to receive in trust, in love and in thankfulness, and to consider the needs of the Earth from which he draws his sustenance. Literally, if he is to continue living upon Earth he must live in a consciousness of Limitless Love and Truth.

This is the essence of Revelation. This consciousness needs to be awakened in man. He needs to shoulder his creative responsibilities and accept his spiritual maturity. This is the point he has reached in the evolution of his Being; this is the New Age. He is not without help in doing this. This new cycle does not spring itself upon him without preparation, a preparation which is the cosmic context behind Revelation. Within man himself and within his world, the Christ has dwelt and worked and built up the patterns of strength and wisdom and new consciousness on which man can now draw. There is no reason for hopelessness, nor for destruction. The new heaven and the new earth exist; they need to be recognized and brought into greater manifestation until the first heaven and the first earth shall have totally passed away. Man need not concentrate on this passing world; the new homeland calls to him. The promised land is spread before him. His changed consciousness is the passage that will take him to it.

Revelation is the breath of the New Age now. There is no waiting. Earth has already passed into the new, taking with it the essence of its past, the wisdom of all that has gone before. The Earth Logos has met his destiny and all his children are now meeting it with him. From the cosmic context, Revelation takes on a very personal aspect. Born from cosmic cycles of time and consciousness, the meaning of Revelation must ultimately resolve itself within the life of each individual. Each of us is the gateway to the New Age. Each of us is the revelator. None of us can escape this. Change is upon us, not the least because of man's own actions. Let this time of Revelation, of cosmic change, truly find fulfilment within us in the birth and nourishment of the new heaven and the new earth. Cosmic destiny awaits!

Chapter 17

The New Culture

The New Age is here now. This is the essential message of Revelation. Earth has entered a new phase of energy expression. It is important to realize that this new pattern of consciousness was not imposed upon this planet from outside. The cosmic energies act only as stimuli to draw forth from within the life of Earth the qualities which, when expressed actively, best complement and blend with those energies. The New Age is a result of education, a drawing out from within. It has always existed in essence, just as future ages, yet to come, now exist as unrealised potentials. Revelation is merely the educational impulse to bring the New Age potentials to the surface, to spark them into expression. There is no conflict with the past, for the past is seen as the womb of the future. The forms in which life has expressed itself in the past may have to change, to expand in order to adapt to the expansion of that life itself, but change of this nature is evolution, growth, not conflict, not opposition. Forms always change, but the essential life within those forms goes on eternally, expanding itself into greater and greater expressions of its intrinsic potentials and characteristics.

The same is true for the individual. For each of us the New Age is here now. It has always been here, our spiritual "genetic pattern" awaiting the proper timing to unfold. Yet, for many of us, the New Age remains only a vision, a dream, something yet to come, if indeed we know anything about the New Age at all. Thus, we have the paradox of carrying around within us the seed, the reality, the life of a new world, a new culture, a new creative explosion of indwelling life, yet actually living and acting attuned to an old world, a limiting culture, and seeing that world as the only reality.

It is to break this paradox, to resolve the energies of the two worlds and to liberate the new world from within each individual, that Revelation manifests. This is the function of

Revelation: to reveal, in whatever form is necessary to impress its message onto human awareness, the energies, the visions, the inspiration, the direction and the stimulus that will catalytically unleash the New Age from within the existing patterns of the world and of humanity. Unless it does this, Revelation has no value in itself. The New Age cannot be grafted onto the world; it must be unfolded from within. Mankind cannot be coerced into building a new culture. It must be inspired to do so. Because of man's free will, the higher dimensions of consciousness, from whence all true revelations flow, can only act through individuals who, in their personal, physical level aspects, have responded to the vision and have released its transforming potentials from within themselves. Each man must choose the direction and attunement which shall guide his life and development.

Thus, in the final analysis, Revelation becomes a very personal matter. Each person must decide inwardly for himself the truth of what any revelation proclaims and if he decides that it is valid, he must act accordingly. He must become the word of Revelation made flesh; he must embody the vision, the inspiration, the direction, and act to release from within himself the new world which Revelation describes. In no other way can Revelation be fulfilled. The whole being must transform itself in orientation to the new vision. Simply to consider it intellectually or emotionally, to treat it on the level of phenomena or words or pleasant hopes, is to miss the point of the Revelation. The energies of the New Age seek complete personal transformation and rebirth, nothing less. The New Age is not a spectator sport. Whatever the cosmic drama behind Revelation may be, for each individual it has value or not, depending on his personal response and understanding and acceptance of a responsibility to allow the energies and visions of Revelation to live in his daily life. For those who do respond to the cosmic picture portrayed earlier in this book, these next chapters will suggest ways in which the meaning of that cosmic context can be realized and released in the context of the personal life, in order to liberate the New Age within the microcosm as it has been liberated in the macrocosm already and to fuse the two together.

The individual and collective task before all who attune to the New Age is to externalize a new culture. This in itself would not be so much of a challenge if man had a clear field in which to work, that is, if he could see clearly the nature of that culture. However, this is not the case. Man lives in a world influenced by many pre-existing patterns of thought and behaviour. Various forces are revealing themselves to his consciousness. Before we can discuss the new culture, we must be aware of some of these forces which may confuse the issue. It is important to remember in so doing, though, that these other influences may be quite valid and proper in their own way and may, in fact, be preparing the way for the full externalization of the new world. We discuss them briefly only to bring the factor of their existence more fully into our awareness. Then we can deal with them while still consistently unfolding the deeper vision of the new culture.

The first of these forces is found in the existence around the world of various archetypal energies expressing themselves around the form of a world-messiah or a new saviour. An example of this is the Christ archetype as manifested in the idea of the Second Coming. We have already discussed the reality of the Second Coming as the unfolding of the indwelling Christ nature within each person in response to a comparable unfoldment of the Cosmic Christ within the etheric energy levels of Earth. It is important to realize here that, in the cosmic context of Revelation, the Christ and the Second Coming and the new manifestation of the Aquarian Christ do not refer to specific people but to universal events and principles manifesting within all life in response to the changes of this new cycle. However, on a personal level within the form-oriented consciousness of mankind, these principles and events may be interpreted differently.

The archetypal Christ simply represents the idea or image of Christ as held by millions of people throughout the world and as enshrined in dogmatic tradition. In the Christian world, this image is generally one of a Saviour, one who leads the church militant against the forces of darkness, a supernatural political power and messiah. As the energies of the Cosmic Christ become increasingly manifest within the etheric life of Earth, many individuals will begin to respond with the realization that the Christ dwells within them. They will feel his presence moving within and through them and will begin to awaken to their heritage of Christhood and Oneness with God, the Beloved. For some of these people, though, this realization will crystallize itself around this archetypal image. They will see themselves as the new saviours, new messiahs, come to establish a new church or to reform the old one. They will see themselves as being the Second Coming personified, fulfilling the work of redemption which Jesus started. If they become caught on this archetypal level, they will be unable to perceive the true nature of the Second Coming as a universal principle at last arising within the majority of mankind, nor will they perceive the new revelations of the Cosmic Christ as he inaugurates the Aquarian dispensation.

However, these people are often performing a service and, in some cases, certain individuals may have taken incarnation for the express purpose of embodying an archetypal pattern (and it should be stressed here that though we have been discussing the Christian aspect, this same phenomenon is occurring in other religions as well, wherever men are looking for a new Divine revelation but are expecting it in terms of the revelations of the past.) By manifesting clearly this archetypal image of a Saviour-Christ come to save souls, these people present this image clearly to mankind. It is brought out of the subconscious of the race into the open where it can be clearly seen and understood and dealt with, a sort of racial psychoanalysis. If this thought-form of what Christ represents demands suffering, repentance and self-abnegation, then this needs to be seen clearly, in contrast to the New Age which represents abundance, love, upliftment of the individual, collective well-being and that sense of inner peace and attunement which releases the individual from the need to suffer. Through this contrast, men can choose their alignments. Do they still deal with the thought-forms and expectations of the old world or can they reorient themselves into attunement to the new life, the new culture, the new characteristics of humanity which seek externalization?

Throughout the world a great sifting is taking place, not between those who are "saved" and those who are "lost", for these are meaningless terms in the light of the Revelation of Limitless Love and Truth, but allowing consciousness to find the level of teaching and activity where they can best be reached by the Christ impulse that seeks to lift all mankind into the New Age. These ones who embody the archetypal thought-forms from out of man's past aid this process. Those who are attuned to those images of the past within themselves are drawn to these various messiahs; there they can receive inspiration and help in a way they can accept in the moment and perhaps they will be uplifted to go beyond that level in due course. Others who feel the stirring of a new culture will not be drawn to such manifestations but will continue to be pulled into those areas or towards those people where the new world is definitely emerging. Thus, there should be no conflict with individuals and movements that proclaim themselves along the lines of past revelations, who seek to capture, in a personal sense, the universality of the Christ impulse; they are performing a task. Yet, they are a force to be recognized, for they test the developing New Age consciousness to see if they truly have the vision of what the Christ represents within the individual and collective destiny of mankind. If a person does not truly know the reality of the Christ within nor recognize the patterns of world unfoldment suggested in the cosmic context of Revelation, his own inner yearning for that presence will influence him to become involved with one or more of these human-level messiahs. Their power should not be underestimated. Attuned to an archetypal thought-form built up by centuries of human thinking and feeling, they can invoke considerable etheric and magnetic power to draw people to themselves and to work seeming phenomena through controlling etheric formative energies. Yet, they are essentially of the old world. The life of the new heaven and the new earth is becoming far more powerful. The future belongs to the new culture.

It will be recognized that the forces which challenge the development of a clear attunement to the thought-patterns of the new culture are fundamentally forces of continuity of cultures and thought-patterns already established on Earth. Through long centuries of tradition, experience, use and familiarity, these cultures have established strong, steady and highly magnetic rhythms of energy. It is ordinarily difficult for an individual to break free of the society and culture and the racial mind into which he was born. Without some kind of help to overcome the inertia of their momentum acting within and upon his consciousness, he will most likely follow the path of least psychic resistance and reproduce in his own life the cultural patterns he has inherited. This holds true especially in relation to the attitudes and ideas which a culture fosters, even if they are of limitation, separation, fear and prejudice. The individual's chances of attuning to and expressing a new culture, a new vision, are generally slim. This is what the pioneers of human consciousness have always had to contend with. Strong souls can manifest their individuality and become the seed-center for the manifestation of a new cultural impulse, but they meet with the resistance of the entrenched establishment, which is the outer plane manifestation of well established thought-forms that resist change. To overcome this, such pioneers have often had to manifest extremes of individuality and selfhood, which create problems of power and authority in their own right. Since one of the characteristics of the New Age is collective and group work, with each individual being uplifted, and since the motion and revelation of the Christ is a universal principle, the day of the strong, dominating individual is past. The pattern for the future is not one of a single person or group leading the rest of humanity into the promised land but of men and women acting through love and truth as a leaven within mankind to stimulate and lift the whole, distributing the arising Christ principle as widely as possible within the race of man. We will speak more on this later.

There are, of course, prominent men and women who so embody the principles of the New Age, of love, of truth, of universality and the nourishment of the Divinity dwelling within all men, that they will be leaders and points around which others who seek to unfold the new culture will collect. In some cases, they may be powerful, even forceful people, but their consciousness will manifest an energy that is freeing to others, not dominating. They will be agents of the whole of Life, not of a particular fragment. To allow these pioneers to do their work without having to attune too much to powerful ego forces in order to contest the established cultural inertia, other energies have entered upon Earth. These are interim forces, often destructive in their expression. They stir a divine discontent within Earth and all its patterns, a yearning for something other than what has been. These are not essentially destructive energies; destruction results when an individual is stirred out of his old pattern but does not find a new pattern to which to attune and, in his frustration, strikes out. These are the forces so much at work within the younger generation over the past decade. By stirring up human consciousness, the rigidity of the old cultural patterns is broken up; it becomes less monolithic. Within this state of unrest and searching for new patterns, the true pioneers of the New Age can concentrate on building the new, allowing the attractiveness of the new to draw more and more people into attunement with it. They do not have to use any of their energies in conflict or destructive rebellion against the old.

However, the old cultural patterns are still strong and highly attractive in their seeming stability and security. This creates a strange phenomenon in which individuals who are dissatisfied with their native land and culture seek to attune not with a new pattern but with another of the already existing cultural consciousnesses. Thus, many young people, unhappy with the materialism and form-orientation of the West, seek to become part of an Eastern cultural and spiritual pattern. However, unless a person, through previous association in other lives, is already highly attuned to the adopted culture, he will find it difficult to blend fully with it. It takes years to cast off the natural psychic rhythms of the society into which one was born and to become one with another society whose culture, thought and feeling patterns have their roots sunk deeply into centuries of time. Thus, many people who are attracted to an adopted culture eventually find themselves part of no culture. Unable fully to throw off the conditioning of their native pattern, unable to penetrate deeply enough to become one with the adopted culture (particularly if it is very different in its basic orientations, such as the differences between the East and West), these people become fully attuned neither to one nor to the other. In some cases, the individual takes only as much from other cultures as he needs to more powerfully resist and express his rebellion against his native pattern. An example of this is the person of the West who studies under an Indian holy man who employs a discipline and a rhythm of life built up over the centuries, practising scrupulous cleanliness and order and peace. The Westerner learns what he wishes and returns to the West, living in an unclean, unwashed, rebellious pattern, expressing inner turmoil. He has only skimmed the surface of a teaching but has not entered the deeper rhythms of the culture that produced the teaching, rhythms which are the very heart and soul of the teaching. This is a form of cultural and psychic rape and applies as well to Easterners who seek to graft the techniques of Western culture to their native land without taking into account the deep rhythms of consciousness which are the source of Western culture.

This is not the place to discuss the relative merits of East and West nor whether there should or should not be separation between them. The new culture embodies the essence of the best of both, the inner attunement of the Orient, the outer creativity of the Occident which gives expression and exaltation to that attunement. In fact, for the new culture there is no difference between inner and outer attunement, for the one life, the whole, the Beloved is to be found in both blended into oneness. The point I am making is that while the new culture is still in its infancy of expression, though it has the power of the future behind it, the older cultures have great attractiveness for people who, stirred up and dissatisfied with their native culture, do not know where to turn. The power of the past is not ultimately stronger than the power of the future, if I may express it in this way, but it can be more attractive initially by virtue of being a known and established pattern. It may not be wholly satisfactory but at least it doesn't hold the terrors of the unknown and the as-yet-unrealized.

There is a third force complicating the issue and making difficult the clear realization and externalization of the new culture. Man, confronted with challenge or frustrated and uncertain where to turn, may seek to run away. This was possible in the past when man had lots of room to expand into and plenty of natural resources to draw upon. Now that luxury is past, which, as we have already seen, is one of the reasons why he must begin to approach his living world with a spirit of Limitless Love and Truth. Yet, the urge to escape is still there. Many people, dissatisfied with the establishment about them, unable or unwilling to adopt a new culture, retreat. They run into psychic realms if they cannot run to new physical ones. This manifests as the phenomenon of addiction.

Addiction is often thought of in terms of drugs and certainly the problem of drug addiction is one of man's major challenges, particularly in the West. The promise of the New Age and the new culture is one of unity, blending the various levels of consciousness into a oneness of effort and expression. It represents the physical, material realm blended with the higher spiritual realms for the greater manifestation of the oneness of consciousness. It most certainly is not a pattern of seeking the higher realms in rebellion or conflict with or escape from the outer physical world. Drugs often are used for just this purpose, in order that the individual can run into a private world of fantasy or at least dull the frustrating impingement of the outer, uncomfortable world. They can also be seriously used as a hopeful means of becoming aware of higher levels in which the individual is not so much running away as seeking something beyond himself. The problem here is that while certain drugs can bring about, for some individuals, an experience of higher levels of consciousness, they do so by separating the being. The chemical releases certain of the higher bodies of consciousness which then rise to their natural levels, transmitting back a more or less clear experience of those levels. The process of attunement in the New Age is actually the reverse of this and involves both raising the lower levels and bringing the higher levels down into a greater blending of oneness. It is a synthesizing, integrating procedure, not a separating one. After taking drugs, the consciousness still has to integrate the experience into the wholeness of the self if it is to have any real value; unfortunately, the effect of the drug is to weaken the integrative powers of the self. This is one reason why taking drugs does not represent a path to the culture and world of the New Age.

Addiction, though, refers to more than just drugs. It is an entire attitude and process of consciousness, representing the increasing dependency of the consciousness on patterns outside itself; it is the search for fulfilment carried out in the wrong places, outside the being rather than within. It also represents a weakening of the integrating, unifying powers of the individual, making it increasingly difficult for him to feel at one and whole within himself and thereby intensifying his search for that wholeness through linking himself with some outside form or power. Addiction is part and essence of the phenomenon of escape. One can be addicted to people, to things, to sports, to literature, to meditation, to "seeking spiritual truths," in short, to anything that will occupy some level or fragment of the self and give the illusion in the moment of "being fulfilled and busy." Addiction is the manifestation of separation, for it represents an exclusive attachment to a part or a fragment of the whole, preventing true integration of the being with the wholeness within itself and in the world from taking place. Such a state makes it more difficult to attune to a culture of the new which is one of unity and wholeness. Also, in an age when, through attunement to the whole of life, man may discover the true purpose and power of his free will and know a new independence within himself, addiction maintains his dependence on powers outside his own Divinity. It emphasizes the feelings of lack and need, while the energies of the New Age come to open man to a new consciousness of abundance.

These three forces, which manifest as the seeking of refuge in archetypal images, in past cultures or in addiction, complicate the arising from within man's consciousness of the full realization of the new cycle of energies which seek expression within him. There are undoubtedly other forces which do this as well, but these three are representative. They possess one characteristic in common; they all manifest a quest outward for fulfilment rather than a going within, and they all manifest a form-oriented consciousness. In the first instance, rather than seeing the Christ as an inner presence as well as an outer one, a universal life unfolding from each individual, the individual looks for the Christ to come in a form external to himself; he looks to another or others to manifest this presence for him. In the second instance, he looks to another culture to satisfy his need, instead of examining the truly creative potentials he has within himself to bring a new culture to birth in harmonious co-operation with others: a new culture which, by blending the best of the past with the living, Divine creativity of the present and the vision of the future, could better fulfil man's present needs of consciousness than any of the older ones can do. Further, unable to become fully integrated into an adopted culture, he may use it simply in protest and rebellion against the society of his birth, as some people seek to pit the subjective, inward-drawing culture of the East against the objective, outward-oriented West, a distinction and a conflict entirely without meaning in the New Age. Thirdly, the individual, unable to recognize wholeness within himself and identifying himself solely with the fragmentary aspects of his being, turns to other forms outside himself to bolster his power and psychic well-being and to attempt to discover the sense of oneness and inner fulfilment, creating a state of psychological and even physical addiction.

If materialism is defined as the obsession with form on any level of being, then these three forces can be seen as the continuation of man's materialistic consciousness. As such, they are highly attractive, for they express an orientation familiar to mankind. If one had to create a new culture in the face of such entrenched and attractive attitudes and forces of mind and emotion, it would be very hard. However, these forces also represent the activity of the interim energies which are stirring up the inner discontent of people and emphasizing their need for greater meaning and fulfilment in their lives. Though, in terms of the New Age, they represent faulty channels for seeking satisfaction of that need, they are a symptom of a positive climate of change and outreaching for new discovery.

The essence of Revelation is that now a New Age has dawned and new channels for answering the needs of man are opening. What is more, these channels do not simply satisfy these needs in a temporary way; by helping an individual to find his inner wholeness, the cause of the need is satisfied. He is freed from the pressure of being a fragment in a world of fragments. He becomes a living wholeness, radiating that regenerative power into his environment. The personal importance of Revelation is that the energy sources of the old world have been cut off; the old world exists by habit. The new culture, the new world is now radiating the most powerful magnetic energies, attracting consciousnesses to itself that it may be externalized and fulfilled in the lives of men and women and all the kingdoms of life. This means that a person who sincerely seeks attunement to the new aligns himself with energies far more powerful than those flowing through the three forces described above. He may have to work to replace habits of thinking and feeling, but he will be assisted in this. Though the forces of past momentum are strong, the forces of creativity releasing the new culture into manifestation are stronger. The forces of the past are basically ideas, which can only be overcome by a stronger idea. It has been said that the strongest force in the world is an idea whose time has come. The time has come for the Idea that is the seed-life on the formative etheric of the new culture, the New Age.

With the initiation of the Earth Logos and the change of energies upon the formative etheric, with the corresponding release of the Christ energies that had entered Earth at the time of Jesus — a release which is the true Second Coming — and with the complementary "descent" to Earth from cosmic levels of the energies of the New Age and their Regent, the Cosmic Christ in his Aquarian dispensation, the Idea of the new world, the new culture, the new heaven and the new earth was energized and became the world of reality. It will manifest itself. This is the promise and the inspiration of Revelation.

Revelation also calls for the lives of individuals to embody this vision, this promise and inspiration, and to give them a chance to work through those individuals' lives. An idea whose time has come may be strong, but it cannot truly flex its muscles until it is given expression through action, through demonstration, through living the life which that idea inspires. The old cultures are strongly attractive because they are manifesting themselves in the actions and demonstrations of millions of lives, yet these cultures can no longer fulfil the expanded needs of man's evolving consciousness. The new culture does exist. It must now be attuned to and allowed expression. The ideas of the new culture must be demonstrated, lived, proven. Then, indeed, no existing power will be able to contest this new world emerging and humanity will have been given a positive vision to move toward.

The reason the three forces described above are so strong is because of the discontent being stirred up by this creative period of time. People are seeking, yet do not know where to find that which they seek except in the established pathways and byways. This is why the present need is for action in order to externalize the new culture, to provide a living, creative, positive alternative to such forces of the past. This is why energies cannot be expended by the pioneers of the New Age on conflict, on rebellion against the old, for these create no new vision, no living force of new culture that can reach the souls of the majority of humanity. Now is the time to realize the vision and to act upon it in order to make it real.

I work through life and through consciousness. Man must believe in me. . . . Then I may be revealed through him, as he is the builder of a new heaven and a new earth. The new heaven and the new earth shall emerge, not in conflict with the old but in revelation of their own being and their own values. The best way (to) help those within the old is to build the new, for then power and light and energy (are added) to those patterns which now represent the salvation and nourishment and growth of this planet into its appointed destiny.

The first vision of Revelation is that the New Age is here now, that it is a real force, a presence, to which one can attune. The Second Coming has occurred and Earth is in readiness to receive the new Christ manifestation. The new culture exists as a reality within humanity and within the world, radiating powerfully the rhythms and vibrations that will characterize it and setting into motion the processes of its externalization. There is no waiting. Now is the time to begin building the new earth, drawing for inspiration, strength and power upon the reality of that earth upon the inner levels of consciousness.

This is the first step, to understand and to accept this vision. This opens the being to the necessary inspiration in the moment, to create the forms that will clothe the vision. The old has held its power because there has been no vision to challenge and replace it. Now that vision is here. As it is increasingly expressed and recognized, it will grow in its ability to draw men to it, to counteract the escape patterns of the past. Building the new indeed is the best help to be given to those caught in the old, for it will give them the direction and hope to move out and become themselves citizens of the new heaven and the new earth. Acceptance, belief, action: these will bring the new culture into being. That culture exists now; it is radiating its influence upon us all. We don't have to fight the patterns of the old in order to be free. Now we can attune to the vision and reality of the new and freedom will be ours. This is the promise of Revelation.

Chapter 18

Seeking the Vision

Man is much, much more than a biological mechanism simply reacting its way through life. Within him flows the creative spirit of life that seeks to go beyond the present form of the world and give birth to new horizons and heights of consciousness. Growth and expansion are the very essence of this spirit and it is nourished by a vision that releases its capacities for growth and gives its life meaning. Man must have a vision of the future that challenges and creatively uplifts him. Without it, he loses touch with his greater life and truly sinks to the level of being merely a biological and psychological machine, reacting automatically to the stimuli of life about him.

We have already discussed that the Christ is the educative force within Creation. He draws out of all form and spirit the greater potentials of Divinity that lie therein. This, in essence, is what vision does for man. It inspires him to draw out his inner strength and courage and creativity and to use them to make the vision real. The Christ is the presence from which vision and revelations come. He releases to mankind the ideas and the inspiration that will lift him and expand his being. Earth, as a living Being and as a collective of many living Beings, is now within a new cycle, a New Age. The visions of the past are no longer sufficient. They are either being reinterpreted or discarded in preparation for new vision. This new vision, this new inspiration, is vital in order to enable the life of Earth to move through all its members in externalization if its New Age forms. In particular, the consciousness of man must be reoriented away from the past into the future and into the present as the creative moment in which the future is realized. Thus, the Christ gives to this cycle the visions that will fulfil the potentials of this cycle, new visions and, in some cases, unprecedented revelations.

It is for this reason that in this book a difference is made between the Second Coming of the Christ and a new manifestation of this same universal presence and impulse, which could be called the Aquarian Christ. There is no essential separation between them, yet one is a manifestation in preparation for the other. The Second Coming is the arising within the world of the Christ life in order to fill the lives of men with sufficient love and goodwill to permit them to receive from the macrocosm and unfold from within themselves the energies and powers and consciousness of the New Age. Further, the concept of the Second Coming is past-oriented for many people. It links the mind with an expression of the past and leads to an expectation of a repetition of that expression. It does not take into full account the possibility of a much greater manifestation of the Christ presence, revealing aspects of Divinity not previously known by man. Indeed, just as Jesus was rejected by many who felt that he did not fit into the classical expectations of a messiah and who could not perceive the fullness of what he represented, so the Christ manifestation for this New Age could go unrecognized and rejected by many who are thinking of a Second Coming as a repetition and reinforcement of the past. We are in a New Age. It is born clothed in the best of the past cycles but it primarily seeks to reveal and to manifest its own new values and culture. We must be prepared for change and for receiving into ourselves the uplifting challenge of the unknown.

We are in a time of Revelation, a time of a manifestation of the eternal Christ impulse. In his aspect, now released from the imprisonment of matter and functioning within the etheric life of Earth, he is the Second Coming, the Resurrection, the impulse of rebirth and regeneration that prepares man to receive him in his further aspect as the source for a new and cosmic vision of Divine life to be realized by man during this Aquarian cycle. To a great extent, this vision has yet to be fully released. We receive now only the beginnings of it, suggestions of the splendor of consciousness into which we move. Yet, even these suggestions are alive with power and inspiration.

This is what is most needed, inspiration that opens a man's heart to his creative attunement with the Beloved, allowing the practical steps of unfolding the New Age vision to be revealed through that inspiration itself. The blueprint of the new culture is not ready-made to be handed to man from higher levels. Man must learn to build that culture through his attunement to the ideas of the New Age, to externalize its characteristics from within his own creative consciousness. In this he will find his new glory and his fulfilment as a builder of a new heaven and a new earth. He does not need detailed plans or techniques, though these may later come and be important. It is vision. It is knowing that the age of man's creative and spiritual maturity is here now, that a powerful and irresistible new life is moving upon Earth, the life and presence of the Cosmic Christ and the vision he inspires.

It is important, at this stage in the externalization of the new culture, not to become too conditioned as to what to expect. The overtones of the past are still strong and can cast confusing shadows on the images of the future. Yet, there are some ideas which are part of the New Age vision that can be discussed, as they may be signposts to the finding of greater vision and revelation within ourselves. The characteristics of the New Age include oneness, education, creativity and the realization of the rhythms of outbreath. These ideas suggest the quality which the new culture will manifest and indicate a direction for personal reorientation of attitudes and actions more clearly to reflect these ideas.

Oneness is a key concept. In a spiritual sense, the world has always been one. All that lives upon it and within it is linked by a common life, a common evolution. This oneness has expressed itself in apparent diversity and separation. In the past, man's cultures, particularly in the West, have accepted this diversity. There has been a particular awareness of a separation between a man's inner, subjective world, the world of his personal identity, and the outer, objective world that forms his environment. The apparent rigidity and definition of solid forms emphasized the reality of a world filled with diverse and separated objects and entities. However, as we have seen, modern scientific research has proven that nothing is truly solid, that all is a manifestation of various patterns of energy in motion, energy linked in subtle ways throughout the universe into a unified field or oneness. Modern communications are also bringing the impact of oneness onto human consciousness. Historically, communications were controlled by geography, and many peoples live their lives out of touch with all the world save for a small portion within easy travelling distance; cultures could develop relatively isolated from one another. This is no longer possible. New techniques of rapid and accurate transmission of information and experience, such as television and radio satellites circling Earth, now overcome geography and practically remove the barriers of time and space between an individual and events or people elsewhere in the world. Strange cultures are brought directly into one's living room, while modern methods of transportation can jet a person around the world in a matter of hours. All of this is to reveal increasingly to man's consciousness that humanity is one people, citizens of one world. Also, ecological research demonstrates the interrelated nature of all life upon Earth, including the apparent non-life of the soil and the mineral kingdom. The chain of life is so intertwined as to be a veritable Gordian knot of interdependency in which the destruction of a simple one-celled creature dwelling in the oceans can have profound effects on human survival, since this organism is a vital link in the process that purifies air and water for continued use. In all these ways, scientific, technological, ecological, man is having the reality of the oneness of life upon this world thrust upon him.

In the new culture, this realization of the oneness of all is a vital characteristic, and the consciousness of the New Age will be one of keen sensitivity to the needs and direction and development of the whole. Here, too, the concept of oneness and wholeness implies the dissolution of the barrier between the individual's inner world and his environment. This does not mean the loss of a private life; it does mean the cessation of conflict between the individual and his environment, for he will understand the subtle links and laws which make his environment a reflection of his own subjective state. In love and attunement, he will be able to blend his inner and outer world so that they express peace and creative power, not conflict. He will see that the whole is as much an inner quality as it is a reality outside himself. This is important, for in the past man has approached the whole, approached the universal life, God, as if it were a thing apart from him, something in his environment rather than a living presence within himself. Also, in his attempts at communal living with his fellow human beings, the concept of working for the good of the whole has also included the concept of self-sacrifice and self-surrender to the whole. This is again inevitable if he sees the whole as having a separate existence from himself, like a state to which he must offer his allegiance. It is only when he realizes that he is one with the whole, that it is indeed his greater Self and that the greatest contribution he can make to it is the joyous blending of his uplifted and Christ-filled personality and Being in loving communion and co-operation with the others who share wholeness with him, that he begins to know oneness.

In short, the concept of oneness is not the opposite of diversity. It represents the realization of a sense of wholeness within the individual so that he can be a synthesizing force amongst the diversity of his environment. He can move in a world of apparent fragments and be aware that each fragment is really part of a greater whole. For example, a human being is more than the personality we see in the moment. He is the procession of his life and experience since birth, he is the pattern of his future seeking proper realization in the present, he is the earthly aspect of a cosmic and Divine life. Though we cannot see this wholeness, this fuller aspect of a person, we can know that it is there and view him accordingly. We may not be able to move in harmony with what he is or what he is doing in the moment but we can be in harmony with the wholeness of which we are seeing only a fragment.

This is the manifestation of Limitless Love and Truth acting within an individual. We think of love as being an action or a force of attraction bringing diverse and separate elements together. We may think of it as a synthesizing or cohesive energy. Oneness is the only reality and diversity is its apparent manifestation. Love is the realization of this. Love is not an action or an energy; it is a vision from which an action can spring. It is a recognition. Two people do not fall in love. They suddenly catch the vision, the realization of their oneness and this vision sets into motion the mental, emotional and physical energies to reflect that essential oneness in the world of form. Again, the vision is the reality, the creative source, while the physical action is the response inspired by that vision. It may be easier to manifest love in one's life if one does not think of it primarily in terms of actions but in terms of vision. One must realize the oneness, the wholeness of which he is a part, and allow that realization to inspire and direct his actions. Then, instead of straining to generate feelings of love, which many people find difficult to do, one releases oneself to the oneness and love that naturally flow between all beings.

Limitless Love and Truth is the reality of what flows and exists between us all. It is a manifestation of the oneness. It is a vision that creates appropriate action in the moment to meet the unique needs of that moment and blend that moment into the wholeness of Divine experience. It is this vision of the wholeness within ourselves and beyond ourselves that we need to catch, for having caught it, it will mold our personal expression after its own image. One cannot create oneness; one can only realize and affirm its existence and reflect its existence within the worlds of diverse forms. One cannot create love in a fragmentary way, though one can create desire. One can realize the oneness we all share and this realization itself is the vision of love that will reflect itself through our actions.

In short, the cultures of the past have tended to see the world as a collection of separate fragments which could be combined in various ways or separated in other ways. The new culture sees the world as a wholeness manifesting as diversity but never losing its essential oneness, a oneness that uplifts the individual as it includes him.

If the concept of the whole is a dominant New Age theme, then two important sub-themes are education and the manifestation of man's creativity, both of which, in the new culture, reflect the concept of oneness. The word *education* itself conveys the sense of awareness of and respect for the infinite potentials within the individual that is so characteristically a New Age awareness, for education means to lead out from within. Obviously this presupposes the existence of something inside to bring out and worthy of being brought out. For centuries the pioneers of advanced human consciousness have recognized the wholeness that is within each individual. They have seen past the fragmentary aspect so magnified by the lenses of space and time and have been aware that within and behind this apparent fragment we call a human being lies the reality of a cosmic consciousness, the very presence of God. It was this realization, as we have described, that gave these great ones their tremendous capacity to love others, indeed to manifest a limitless and universal love, for they saw clearly the wholeness of the individual and knew him as the manifestation of a process of Divinity. The might not approve of or like the particular action or attitude of that individual within the limited stage of space and time, and their consciousness of truth and discrimination might lead them to act creatively in order to correct behavior that was out of balance. Yet, this did not diminish their love, for their love was not based on the level of the fragment and its actions but on the realization of the whole and the process of Divine externalization that is the essence of the individual. Each of us is a dynamic process of God revealing himself. It is this process, this presence of oneness moving within form, that can be loved, even though a temporary expression of that process may be seen as out of balance and may need to be adjusted.

It was this same realization, that each individual represents a changing reflection into a moment of time of a Divine process of unfoldment, that led to the true concept of education as held by the advanced consciousnesses of the past. Education was the art of assisting this process of unfoldment from within and was based on the knowledge that whole universes were contained within the individual seeking release and unfoldment. It is a manifestation of the Christ impulse, as we have seen. The orientation of education was one of moving from within outward, not one of filling the inner man with stuff from the outside. Teaching was seen as only an aspect of education; the imparting of information and knowledge, while often useful as a catalyst to creative unfoldment, was not as important as assisting the individual to realize and express his wholeness. Rather than seeing the individual as an empty vessel waiting to be filled by experience, the wise ones of the past saw him as a dynamic centre of creativity seeking to externalize itself in continual new life and requiring assistance in gaining the skills to do so. The imparting of these skills and knowledge could only be to help the process of inner unfoldment. Teaching had to respect and acknowledge what was already there awaiting release within the individual and could not obstruct or take precedence over that release. The perspective had to be there. A teacher had to see himself more as a midwife assisting a birth process than as a fountain of knowledge and wisdom from which others must partake. Rather than use his greater knowledge to project himself and make his students copies of himself, he had to use his skills and wisdom to assist each student to be his own master, to find his true individuality and fulfilment. Education had to be freeing, not restricting. The individual was important because each individual represented a unique demonstration of Divinity. This the educator had to realize and respect.

A fragmented world thinks in terms of limits, because fragments have limits. A world that is attuned to wholeness knows no limits, for wholeness is limitless. In a materialistic society, each individual is seen as limited by time, space, his body, his environment: in short, by all the forms that encompass him. His isolation and separation are magnified. Wisdom, knowledge, ability are seen as things apart from him, things which the society must impart to him through education. Education becomes the means of conditioning people to harness their fragmented lives into combinations useful to the whole of society. Its end achievement is to make the individual more dependent and less unfolded, less his own master, less able to act creatively toward the challenges of his environment. This kind of education keeps people on the level of being fragments, dependent on other fragments. True education gives the person his sense of wholeness, of being attuned to a universal life, of being part of the universe and not in conflict with it. By lifting his awareness beyond the concepts of space and time and form, he is initiated into a realization of his limitless potentials, a knowledge that he can do or be anything he chooses to unfold from the infinite within himself.

A materialistic or form-orientated society thinks in terms of working from the outside in. It does not readily conceive of a "withinness" to things; instead, it thinks of manipulating things by applying force or pressure or energy from the outside. It is very aware of inertia, the resistance of form to outside pressures, and thinks in terms of overcoming it. Such a society is manipulative. Nothing would be done unless pressure were applied to get it done. Such a society or culture does things to things, rather than allowing things to unfold, knowing that they will unfold, and providing such assistance as to insure the most perfect unfoldment.

The concept of education is part of the new culture because it most adequately expresses the orientation of that culture. It means something far broader than learning or schools. It means the whole understanding of the reality of the life within all form seeking unfoldment. It does not respect the presence of power that can be applied from the outside to get things done but the presence of inspiration that can summon the power of creative accomplishment from within form. It is not a manipulative culture. It does seek to create channels for the

197

best unfoldment of the Divine potentials within the planet and within humanity. In the analogy of the garden, the old pattern was one of man imposing his will upon Nature through force and manipulation, acting upon the outward form of plants to make them conform to his ideas. The new culture replaces this by recognizing and respecting the intelligence and Divine life seeking to unfold from within the form and providing an opportunity and environment in which that force from within can express in ways suitable to man and plant.

In short, it is a culture that seeks to work with the forces of evolution, not against them, in order to understand the direction of the whole of planetary life and to assist that direction. In this, man attains his true role, that of being headmaster to the planetary school. All kingdoms of life are under his stewardship. He must plan his own activity so as best to fulfil that stewardship. This is true in his dealings with his own kind. He knows the power of the life seeking to unfold; that inner force is not like an object whose inertia must be overcome. It is a joyous arising. Given a chance, it sweeps up through an individual, stimulating him into new creativity and uniting him with the whole. Man must now learn that art of love and education which inspires people to give their own inner life a chance to express itself. We are all educators to each other and to the world, just as we, in turn, are being inspired into greater unfoldments by the Christ and other Beings beyond us in evolution. We each represent the Christ to the world, as we can assist the unfoldment of the Divine Life within and through the forms of the world. In this, we manifest a new aspect of Divinity, for this educational relationship does not fit into the classical esoteric tradition of being either a primal male or a primal female polarity, a positive or negative pole. To educate is neither to give nor to receive. It is to be and in that being, to inspire a comparable unfoldment from within others. Whereas the traditional concept of the father-mother aspects of God expresses the creative relationship that produces form, the educational relationship is the magnetic impulse that draws the creative spirit out of form into greater heights of transcendent expression. It keeps the creative spirit flowing, not allowing it to settle and stagnate into form. It is the relationship based on the recognition that each of us is a manifestation of a wholeness seeking expression, that this process can be trusted, and that the highest service we can perform is to assist that process within ourselves, within others and within the world.

As man continues to grow in his recognition of what is within himself, he will increasingly realize that the creative source of his world is indeed in his own consciousness. Whatever conditions he creates within himself subjectively are bound to reflect outward and to manifest in his environment. The conflict so many feel with their environment is due to the conflict they feel with themselves. Again, this emphasizes the importance of seeing the concept of attuning to the whole not as an outer action as much as an inner orientation. A person at peace with himself projects peace into his environment. A person at one with himself is at one with his environment.

This separation in consciousness between an individual and his world will be replaced in the new culture. The more he realizes that his skin does not really separate him from that world, the more an individual will begin to realize his true creative power. He will not simply react as the environment stimulates him to react when he knows that he can act upon himself and, by changing his consciousness, change his outer conditions. Jesus said that as a man thinks, so he is. This is the principle. The microcosm of the inner life moves to the same rhythms and knows the same energies that flow through the macrocosm. In the knowledge of the oneness, one sees that the inner and outer worlds are truly one. A man may feel helpless to change his world when he looks at it purely from its form aspects, from the outside in, so to speak. The best he can often conceive of is to develop enough force and pressure successfully to contest that world. When a man knows the reality of the power within his consciousness to create inner changes, then he can make those personal changes, knowing that they will be positively reflected into his environment. The macrocosm will manifest the images of the microcosm and vice versa.

The important concept here is that the liberation of man's creative potentials depends on his capturing the vision of the oneness, that he is linked to limitless Divine life and that he doesn't have to act with pressure or force or strain upon his world. He simply has to express, within himself, attitudes and a consciousness that embody the states he wishes his environment to manifest to him and then allow the subtle energies of his new inner orientation to work through him to change his world. In short, whatever a man wishes his world to be for him, that he must be within himself.

In the past, man has often known the diversity and separation of the physical world and has sought to find the oneness. In so doing, he has developed techniques, especially in the East, of going within and finding that state of oneness However, much of that culture was developed at a time when man desparately needed to counterbalance the downward pull of the materializing forces. He had to learn to retreat inward and attune strongly to the realms of spirit. There was also a need for this energy of consciousness to be directed inward and upward in order to build and later to maintain the link that the Buddha and Jesus used to contact and draw down into incarnation the power of the Cosmic Christ. In the Christian dispensation of the West, as well, the concepts of sin and "the fall" led to a consciousness of conflict between the realms of spirit and the realms of matter, manifesting in the need of the soul to choose one over the other. The image of wholeness, of the oneness, of the Christ, of Spirit, of God became seen as the opposite of diversity, distinctness, matter, form.

In the New Age, this conflict must be broken down. The oneness is not a realm different from the physical. God moves and has his being within this lower level of consciousness as much as within any other. Man must learn to find wholeness within himself and then to manifest that reality out into his physical world. The educational impulse of the Christ is helping him to do this, for it is drawing out of him the potentials of the infinities within him. Yet, man must play an active role as well. He must attune to this new vision, attune to Limitless Love and Truth, attune to the new culture as it exists upon the formative etheric. Before we discuss the nature of this attunement, however, there is one other aspect of the New Age vision to consider.

The process of seeking the oneness mentioned above, in which the individual goes within and, drawing his attention away from the outer worlds of form, seeks to rise to a higher level, is symbolically (and sometimes by actual technique) a process of inbreath. Inbreath is a drawing inward. This process describes well the orientation of man for centuries in both his physical and spiritual life in general. He has sought to draw life and its expressions into himself. He has been a centre that pulls inward. This has its positive aspects in the upbuilding of his being, but it has its negative aspects as well. It leads him to orient his attention outward on what is coming to him from his environment rather than on what is creatively seeking expression from within himself. He is aware of the responses which the environment draws from him through reaction, but a reaction is not the same as a creative impulse that releases the gift of his unique Divinity out into the whole.

This tendency towards inbreath, on all levels, complicates a man's ability to realize the existence of a New Age now. He wants to be told what to do, how to do it and when. All this information is there, of course, but waiting to be externalized from within himself through his attunement to his Christ Being. People are waiting for an external force or presence to bring to them the Christ, the New Age, whatever it may be, so that they can breathe it into themselves. They want the oneness, the wholeness to impress itself upon them.

Fortunately for man's greater glory, the New Age and the new culture are not to be imposed by outer forces. They are going to be drawn out of the womb of centuries of preparation and growth on a planetary and an individual scale. Just as the etheric earth was built up until the day of its activation, so has each man over the centuries been building, to some degree, a consciousness, an inner body of mind and heart that is attuned to the qualities and requirements of the New Age. The impact of the initial energies of the Aquarian Christ is to stimulate this New Age body into active life within the consciousnesses of as many men and women as can accept it. We are not called upon to build a new culture, a new civilization, from nothing; it has already been built in essence. Now we must allow its reality to flow through us into manifestation.

This is a process of outbreath. It is a release of ourselves and our love into the world. Instead of drawing back from the world in search of a spiritual peace and oneness, one breathes through action one's own inner peace and oneness back into the world. One learns to work creatively with form in a way that releases from matter the potentials of the Divine life, such as beauty, perfection and inspiration. The new culture is one of taking the riches of the inner life, of high spiritual consciousness, and instilling them into the earth. The rhythms of outbreath imply a shift in consciousness from looking to the environment as a source of supply for things or ideas to satisfy inner lacks, to looking within to the abundance of inner creativity as a source to satisfy the needs of the outer world of form. Just as the Spirit of God moved through chaos and brought about creation, so the Spirit of God within man moves through the world of diversity and form and brings about creative synthesis.

It helps, in this orientation of consciousness, if we do not think of the Divine as a Father who is an outside source from which we can get things, for this is still a consciousness of inbreathing, of drawing things inward to a personal centre. Instead, we may think of him as the creative life within us, and we may think of the world and all it contains as being the Beloved. The Beloved suggests one to whom we may give, one with whom we may unite, and the New Age is definitely the cycle of man's complete unity with the reality of God. Outbreath is the process of mingling our breath with the breath of the world. Oneness is the art of mingling our wholeness within with the wholeness of creation. The flow is outward.

Actually, circulation is vital. There must be an incoming flow as well as an outgoing flow, but man's consciousness has so emphasized the consciousness of receiving (even giving in order to receive, breathing out in order to breathe in) that the opposite rhythm needs to be pointed out. In essence, however, there is no separation. Outbreath, the motion of my consciousness out into the whole in awareness of that whole, is only the primer that activates the rhythms of oneness within me. Then I am essentially neither a giver nor a receiver. I am an educator. I am a centre from which may pour the energies that inspire the unfoldment of new life from old forms. I may manifest at one moment in receiving, then later in giving, but as I am centred in being what is needed by the moment, I am flexible.

As a culture, we have fallen into the habit of sitting and waiting for our leaders to offer to us the materials of life which we need or think we need. Even those who claim to be pioneers of the New Age are often manifesting a rhythm of inbreath. They go to lectures, to conferences, to meetings, to discussions, to meditation sessions, to books; they take in and take in and take in until many of them can discuss most learnedly the New Age and all it will offer. Few are actually attempting to create that New Age in practical action either in their own lives or in society. They await some event that will make it easier for them, an event that will "usher in" the new cycle. They fail to realize that the New Age is a living presence within them seeking externalization. It is like a holy breath within their lungs waiting to be breathed forth upon the clay of a world which might then take on new life.

Learning is important, discussion is important, but we harken back to the idea of education. The motion of the new culture is to inspire the unfoldment from within, not to impose more from without. Inbreath has its place, but outbreath is the key to attunement and true attunement is the key to the New Age.

Chapter 19

Attunement

For the individual, the concept of a New Age may be almost too staggering. He immediately begins to think in physical terms: what kinds of cities will there be, what kinds of schools, what kinds of politics, what kind of society and so forth. We have discussed some of the aspects of the New Age vision which may suggest some answers to this. However, the personal context of Revelation is that the New Age is fundamentally a change of consciousness from one of isolation and separation to one of communion, attunement and wholeness. This change has already occurred within the world consciousness; now, it must be matched by a complementary change in personal consciousness.

All things proceed from consciousness. The New Age is within us. It is not coming tomorrow. It is here now. This is the essence of Revelation: that there is now a presence of new life, new culture, new promise active in the world. The individual does not have to struggle to create a new world. He simply must learn to attune to the reality of the new world which is already here and manifesting its energies about us. Then, through that attunement, he changes his personal consciousness and becomes increasingly part of the rhythms of the new cycle. In this way, he leaves one world and enters another, for with a personal change of consciousness, his personal abilities, friends, environment and everything else will alter to reflect the new energies flowing from and through him. God is the center from which the New Age is emerging and he is within each of us. The creative energies that will bring the new culture into manifestation are flowing from within each of us.

This is the message of Revelation: we are now the builders of a New Age. We are called upon to embark on a creative project, not to destroy, not to rebel, not to retreat, but to attune to the new life within us and release its creative impulse in co-operation with others in order to reveal the new heaven and build the new earth. How? How to do this? The answers are within us. Some help is given from time to time from sources outside ourselves, but this is the age of man's expansion into true God-like creativity, in which he must learn the reality of God's direction within himself. Man is a creative source. He is Divine life unfolding itself. He is surrounded, as well, by that same life moving within the evolution of the whole and to this he can attune for the inspiration he needs to build the new earth.

Attunement is a concept based on oneness and is sometimes expressed as "at-one-ment". It means the expression of that rhythm of outbreath and action that links us, through resonance, with energies and consciousness of a higher spiritual level. It is founded on the realization that there is no real separation between what is within us and what is manifesting in the macrocosm about us. The microcosm of our own being duplicates in all essential aspects the vaster realms of life and consciousness.

We would like to have communication with the Divine, with the Spirit of the New Age, with Limitless Love and Truth, in order to receive concrete directions. In the old culture, communication is looked upon as an exchange of messages between two separated points or entities. Even prayer and worship are thought of as an exchange between man and God, the two being separate. It is this fundamental assumption of division, with its concomitant aspects of conflict, misunderstanding and non-communication, that so characterizes the old world. In the new culture, the fundamental acknowlegement is of unity and oneness, though not necessarily sameness, by any means. It is the awareness of man's powers of synthesis, to work with and blend divergent patterns together and become a master of diversity through being centred in his own consciousness of wholeness. Communication becomes communion.

Attunement is a process of active communion and practical realization of the fact of oneness. It operates according to the law of resonance which states, in this case, that any energy or quality expressed within the microcosm sets up a comparable expression of the same energy or quality within the macrocosm, linking the two together and making them one. We can draw an illustration of this from music. *Middle C* and its first harmonic, which I shall call *high C*, are the same tonal quality but separated by an octave of energy. The two notes played in the same way possess equal amplitude but a different frequency of expression. The higher note is moving faster as a sound wave, hence we hear it as a higher pitched sound. Though most people can differentiate between *middle C* and its higher harmonics, they are still the same note and occupy the same tonal position in the scale. Because of this, whenever one *C* is struck, the other *C's* of higher octaves resonate in harmony and can be heard by one whose ear is sensitively trained.

Likewise, the qualities to be manifested in the world by the New Age also exist within us, though on a symbolically lower octave. If we manifest those qualities within ourselves and breathe them out into our world through action and demonstration, then the higher octaves of these qualities within the macrocosm resonate and express as well. For example, if an individual manifests a true love feeling beyond the level of simple desire energy, an outflow of his being to another or to the world with no expectation of attracting something to himself, then there is a thrill of resonance throughout the universe of the love quality on all its levels of expression on all the octaves of being. His own love flow is augmented and he finds himself attuned, if only briefly, with the presence of love in the universe. He is not contacting that love; he has, through his own action, expressed it and thereby dissolved the barrier between himself and love. He is at one with love.

If I express a quality, then I am that quality. I am one with it. If I express a vision, then I am that vision. I am one with it. If that quality or vision also exists as a living force in the macrocosm, then I become at one with it there, as well, and can find myself being lifted into expressing greater aspects of that quality or vision than I could have conceived of before. Many people, in seeking to understand the New Age, try to grasp what it is and what it will bring ahead of time; in so doing, they often only project the shadows of their own past or desires or fears onto the screen of the developing future, which only confuses the issue.

The New Age exists in the mind of the Cosmic Christ who is its overlord; from him project those energies which shall bring the characteristics of the New Age into form. These same energies exist within the individual and can be tapped by seeking consciously and to the best of one's ability to manifest those qualities and aspects of the New Age vision as we can now understand, such as those we discussed in the previous chapter. We then link up with the macrocosmic ideas and forces and receive the rhythm of knowing which gives us guidance. This is truly living in the moment. It is also working on the planes of form to invoke through resonance the energies of higher dimensions.

This is an important point. In the past, men have often left the planes of form to ascend in consciousness to the higher levels, a form of inbreathing, as we have seen. But the qualities of the higher levels exist on this lower level of consciousness, as well, on a lower octave of energy, just as the quality of *high C* exists in the sound of *middle C*. If I play *middle C*, I am, in essence, playing *high C*, too. People strain after abstract concepts such as "loving mankind" and miss the practical need of loving the specific individuals whom they meet daily. Yet, by expressing a love for these individuals, in the sense of recognizing and respecting the wholeness which they represent, a person attunes to the universal presence of love and allows it to express as well. The Christ indicated this when he said that as goodness was done to the least of his children, it is done to him as well and through him to the whole of life. Attunement works on the principle of finding the microcosmic equivalent of a macrocosmic energy or idea and putting it into action. This releases the energies to which the macrocosmic aspect can resonante.

This is why outbreath is the key to attunement. Attunement is not meditation, although meditation can be an important adjunct. Attunement is based on action, the flow of the being outward to unite and work creatively with his world. It is based on the idea that if I express a principle, then there is no separation between my self and that principle and I am one with all the octaves of expression of that principle, for oneness is oneness. If I only think about expressing a principle, then there is separation. Thinking about something is not the same as expressing it actively. Meditating on being a loving person is not equivalent to actually being a loving person. Indeed, many people have difficulty in achieving anything concretely beneficial out of their meditations and periods of silence because they do not have the balance of putting the energies of their life into creative expression and action. They inbreathe but they do not outbreathe. This increases their separation, whereas outbreath, union, communion with the life about us increase our sense of oneness.

The more we realize that the New Age is here now and this vision lives within us, the more we express ourselves accordingly. We manifest the qualities of the new culture as best we can understand them. We discard patterns of hatred, fear, prejudice, separation, guilt, poverty of vision and all the rest of it and we begin actively to express within ourselves, to our world and to those around us the qualities of love, truth, Light, understanding and abundance. We are not alone. If we become stuck at one level of the vision, someone will come to show us the next step, just as we can inspire those less unfolded than we.

Man's creative spirit in action creates attunement. This is not just physical action; it is action on all levels. We think, feel and move as New Age men and women. We realize that the world is a creative adventure and we approach it accordingly, not limiting ourselves to the forms of the past but using the dynamics of the present moment to blend past wisdom with future inspiration into a fusion of present creativity. Then, by expressing our own creativity, our own powers of externalizing something of ourselves into the world rather than simply reacting to the world, we attune to and become one with the forces of cosmic creativity, that represent the cosmic context of Revelation, and the universal sources of the new culture and the New Age.

Always, then, in discussing Revelation and the New Age, we come back to the point that this is a time for doing, for demonstration. If a person wants to know more about the new culture, wants to be part of it, then let him begin to express himself now in the best way he can according to the vision of that culture, knowing that he will then attune to the forces which are externalizing that culture, giving him greater revelation within himself. Man cannot run from his world. He must reveal the wholeness, the Light, the love, the creative power within himself and blend these qualities into the world.

This is attunement. One acts to express the qualities of universal life as he finds them in his microcosmic world. Then, by the laws of attraction and resonance, he becomes one with the macrocosmic equivalents of those qualities and adds to his individual life the power, the guidance, the wisdom of the whole. Attunement is not communication with something outside and separate from ourselves. It is the breathing of our true selves out into the world and finding, in the revelation of that breath, that the world and we are One. Attunement is not a technique as much as it is a principle, a manifestation of the reality of oneness. As we understand and manifest that principle, we shall truly be builders of the New Age.

Chapter 20

Building the New Age Now!

The new heaven and the new earth are forming in your midst. What I am is not a form. I am life and the spirit of life. My new heaven and new earth emerge throughout the world. . . . The choice is not between forms but between consciousnesses. What I am cannot be resisted. If I live within [people], I will direct them. I can work in an office, in a factory, in a school, in a temple, in a church, in a mine; I can work anywhere and be anywhere, for I am in all places. If (people) attune to what I am, they will find that I propel them perfectly beyond all forms that would encase them and leave them in the old. Thus, if it is deemed wise for you no longer to remain in patterns of the old world, you will be withdrawn to other patterns, such as into a New Age centre. Always be prepared for change. All who are of me will eventually commit themselves to the building of the new, no longer in conflict with the old, no longer in revolution.

The New Age is here now. The forms that will express it on the physical level are beginning to take shape here and there about the world, forms built by men and women who have caught the vision of Revelation that a new world is at hand. These are not necessarily people who are expressing some extraordinary consciousness of cosmic illumination; for the most part they are very ordinary-seeming people who realize that the patterns of the old world spell death and that the hope of humanity lies in bringing to birth a new vision. Yet, in their willingness to throw off apathy and the paralyzing thought that an individual is powerless to affect the forces of disintegration abroad in the world, these men and women are truly manifesting a cosmic presence. They are the embodiment of man's true destiny; they work to reveal to him the gift of Divine creativity that is his heritage. They demonstrate that there is no power greater than an individual attuned to the wholeness of life, to the God of oneness.

This is the impact of Revelation: promise, hope and inspiration, the inspiration to do something in one's own life to manifest a New Age consciousness. The New Age is consciousness first, form later. Yet, even the forms are beginning to take shape. Here and there throughout the world people are gathering together in communities to explore new patterns of culture and human relationship, to anchor the vision of the New Age through practical life and demonstration. Others, living in the "old world," are learning to rise above the pressures of modern society, to become centers of peace and stability and new hope in a world that is falling to pieces. This is truly living the life of Revelation.

Between the developing New Age centers and the center of New Age consciousness within each individual are strong and subtle bonds. As the outer communities grow and develop, so is the power of individual builders strengthened. As individuals attune to the rhythms of the new culture, it is not at all unlikely or unusual for their lives to change in a natural way to guide them out of patterns of instability and into forming communities. For a time, these communities may appear isolated; they need breathing time in order to establish themselves, to anchor deep in the work and hearts of their members the rhythms of the new. Yet, when these energies are anchored, then are the gates opened. The new culture shall spread, for the future is on its side.

Throughout the world thousands of men and women are attuning to the promise of Revelation and learning to change themselves more adequately to express that promise in their lives. Through their efforts, the new culture is manifesting in thousands of small yet important ways. Their example is having an impact on consciousnesses around them, indirectly attuning them to the new. Who can estimate the importance of this?

The point is that the New Age is here. True energy and powers of rebirth have been released upon Earth. Change is occurring. This is not an abstract concept. It is the manifestation of a new heaven and a new earth, and it builds itself and forms itself in the midst of the old. In time, even now in fact, these thousands of separate individuals and centers become linked on the outer, even as they are already linked in the oneness which the presence of the Cosmic Christ demonstrates. Then the demonstration of the new culture will be even more apparent and irresistible.

This is the true personal context of Revelation. The words of Limitless Love and Truth are more than just words or strange concepts. They are realities that are being felt and experienced and expressed by men and women throughout the world, of all cultures, of all races, of all religions, bound together by their common attunement to a vision of a new world for man, a world of beauty, of promise, of creative power, of love and the presence of the Beloved. These people are attuned because they are acting in their lives to create this world and they express the motives and attitudes of the new. They are not in direct conflict with the old; they are not in rebellion. They are discovering the power of their creativity linked to the life of God and they are manifesting that discovery. They seek to build new communities where the New Age culture can be purely explored and anchored or they remain in the by-ways of the old world and seek to build the new vision of Love and Truth and creative, positive action into the consciousnesses of others who share that world with them but live in hopelessness and poverty of vision and form. These people know the presence of the new that moves with them wherever they are and they know that, if necessary, they can be moved even more fully into the forms of the new culture by being guided to help build the many communities now forming.

In a world filled with thoughts of death, decay, destruction and despair, the promise and vision of Revelation, no matter what form or words it takes, stand out like a fiery beacon into a new world. "Arise," it says, "and listen. Cast off your tatters of consciousness and know the new that seeks birth within you. It unfolds around you. Take comfort from this and do not

212

feel alone. The world moves into a new cycle. Come forth, you builders, and build the new heaven and the new earth."

The New Age is not a spectator sport. It is not something we can receive. Instead, strengthened and uplifted by the release of the Christ impulse upon the earth and the increasing manifestation of the Aquarian Christ, we are asked to give forth from our own beings the essence and the form of this new culture and new world. For ages man has looked outside himself for what he receives, not knowing that he draws all things to him by the quality of his own consciousness. Now he is being directed within to know the promise, the hope, the creativity that is within him, and he is being asked to release these qualities through positive action into his world. Revelation is not a great Being telling man what to do. It is his own being seeking to release itself. It is his own personal and collective future asking to be admitted into his present. It is his own New Age seeking to blend with the New Age of others to create a new heaven and a new earth. Limitless Love and Truth is his own Divine nature speaking to him, calling forth the promise within him. Man himself is Revelation; the continuance and unfoldment of Revelation is now up to him.

Part IV
Revelation 1975

Chapter 21

California Contact

Revelation is not just what is contained in this book. It is a spirit of transformation, revisioning and creativity moving through many people and groups throughout the world. It takes a variety of forms but generally fulfills a certain pattern or quality of thought and expression, as I have suggested. Growth, love, wisdom, skill in action, attunement to the whole of life, synergy, holism, communion . . . all of these suggest the nature of that spirit. Not all alleged New Age movements express these qualities; some, unfortunately, continue to manifest separatism, competition, spiritual authoritarianism and arrogance. By the same token, there are organizations, groups and individuals who are not identified as being "New Age" and who may not even be familiar with that term who are nonetheless expressing this spirit of wholeness as best they can.

Findhorn is one of the finest New Age centers I have personally contacted. It was a joy for Myrtle and me to live and work there, a creative privilege for which we are grateful. However, just as revelation is not contained in a book, so it is not held only in one place or time. For all our attunement to Findhorn and our creativity with Peter and Eileen, the time came when we needed to return to the United States and attune to the spirit of revelation here and in other parts of the world. In the spring of 1973, we came back to California, where we had worked in our pre-Findhorn days.

With us came a number of other Americans who had been working with us in the community, as well as a Yogoslavian, an Englishman and Dorothy Mclean, who also felt that her time at Findhorn had come to an end, at least for a time. Together we formed the Lorian Association to be a non-profit, educational vehicle for whatever expression the spirit of the new might wish to take with and through us. In time, we realized that for awhile at least that expression did not involve setting up a community ourselves but in assisting the unfoldment within this country and with other countries of a network of groups, individuals and centers that were identifying with the New Age idea. At times, we worked as a group, invoking and embodying a collective energy of service, which we poured into workshops, conferences, concerts, the creation of a record album of songs we had composed, titled *Winds of Birth*; at other times, we found it best to disperse, to withdraw our collective energies and concentrate on individual patterns and responsibilities: jobs, families, and the like. Throughout this process, which continues even as I write this, we have been learning what it means to embody revelation with focus and fluidity, with form and with formless attunement. We have been enriched by the extent to which others are also sharing this process and learning.

During this period, which for me has been dominated by the work on my book, *Emergence*, the work which Myrtle and I have done has also been evolving and changing with growth. In this connection, we have often been overlighted by our friend, John, though we have just as often been left on our own. It has always been the policy of the Beings I have worked with on other levels not to tell us what to do but to share perspectives with us and help us to help ourselves. We are responsible for our actions on this level; we must make the decisions, not them, but they are often available to help that decision-making process.

Around New Year's Day, 1975, I began feeling the approach of a more powerful energy from other levels than I had felt for some months. This continued for several days. Then, on January 8th, I felt John about, and Myrtle and I sat down to have a session with him. His identity was strongly represented, and I had little trouble in communing and blending with him. I found, however, another presence there, too, a familiar one which I had not felt in that manner for some time: Limitless Love and Truth. Since I have always believed this to be a universal principle, as I described in this book, I have always felt its presence as a quality; I was surprised, however, to once again find that quality personifying itself enough to make a contact.

John spoke first, describing the nature of the Limitless Love and Truth phenomenon now and in 1970. This was by way of introduction. He then gave way, and I found myself again transmitting words formed by the impact of that universal quality upon my person, guided by the particular image it sought to communicate.

The next two chapters are the transcripts of these two communications.

Chapter 22

John: A Description of Limitless Love and Truth

January 8, 1975

I bless you and extend to you each the love of God. I am John. That presence which seeks entry to communicate with you may be looked upon as a continuation of a process or stream of energy which externalized itself through the Limitless Love and Truth transmissions several years ago. At that time, that process entered within the conditions that were available to it, both within yourselves and within the environment of Findhorn. It encountered certain thought forms in that environment and sought to use those thought forms as a tool in its own communication. Thus, it appropriated the identity of Limitless Love and Truth, partly because those terms symbolize its own quality and message and partly because that identity lay at the foundation of certain of the energies of Findhorn's beginnings.

There existed a network of energy gathered around the thought form of Limitless Love and Truth which contributed to the founding energies of Findhorn. To some extent, this network was limited and tied to certain conceptions of the past, particularly with respect to the idea of Limitless Love and Truth and the inauguration of a New Age. Findhorn drew support from this network, from the consciousnesses of the people within it, and it was deemed necessary — if a proper alignment was to be made between Findhorn, its supporters, and the newer energies that sought entry into that center as part of its unfoldment — to reach back into Findhorn's past and the past of this network to revivify the image of Limitless Love and Truth and to draw it forward under a new sponsorship and presentation. By this action, the guiding forces concerned hoped to release an energy that was being limited and also to express a new image relating to the New Age and its unfoldment within humanity.

A seed was planted at that time concerning the nature and function of Limitless Love and Truth as an archetypal force within humanity and within the world. Now it is the desire of this process to add to that seed and to present a message that will take its place with the earlier ones.

This process or presence does not fit any of the usual images that men have to describe a source of communication. It is not a Being; it is not a personality; it is not the Christ. It is not God. It incorporates and is blended with the essence of many Beings and ultimately of all Beings. It is of the Christ and is an expression of Divinity. In its communication with you this day through the focus of your consciousnesses, it partakes of the energies of your higher selves (David & Myrtle), your minds and hearts, and of the energies of others who, though not physically present, attune to your focus. It draws on the planetary network of world servers which exists on the inner and which is in the process of externalization onto the outer planes. It draws on myself and on others greater than I. In short, this presence is a number of things as it seeks sufficient personification to address you; perhaps it could be called not only Limitless Love and Truth but the presence of the indwelling self of humanity, seeking to address its energies in a particular way at this time through an image of a New Age which represents another stage in the process of that self's unfoldment through history. Thus, we could call this presence the spirit or image of the New Age.

Limitless Love and Truth, though, is an adequate description of its intents and thus of its identity, but care must be taken that it is not identified as a Being and that any form of external projection of this energy on the part of men into the image of an entity, permitting an upsurge of devotion towards and the creation of a cult around that image, does not take place. If we use the term, "Limitless Love and Truth," as a point of contact to identify this presence, then this is not to refer it necessarily to what has gone before but to refer it to qualities of life and consciousness which are the hallmark of the New Age emergence.

The challenge in communication is that this is a diffused energy field which is potent but insubstantial by your standards. It must be given sufficient concrete imagery for your minds to blend with it in concrete communication. Therefore, we must create a thought form through which it can make contact with you, yet this cannot be too concrete lest it personify this energy too much and throttle its proper entry by making it appear that it is an exterior presence separate to yourselves and to the lives of human persons.

Perhaps a useful image, then, is that this is the Deva of the New Age. It is that which embodies the blueprint or the ensouling energy for this new cycle. It enters to assist a greater life flow emerging from the divine image of the earth and the divine image of humanity to come together and to express in a particular synthesis at this time. We may draw an analogy from nature: the seed in the soil contains within itself a source of emergence which we are calling an image. This image encompasses all that is contained within the life cycle of that plant. It is not an image specifically of the seed, of the shoot, of the stem or flowers or of future seeds. The image is of that which is the life, the meaning within creation, the potential, the idea which, in its stages of externalization through time, adopts these various specific forms of seed, stem and flower as part of the process of its being. The image itself is outside of time; time, in a sense, orients itself to receive this image and to reflect it in the various stages of itself, a reflection you would call "its becoming."

If you could perceive this image directly rather than sequentially through its becoming, it would be as if you could see at once the entire life cycle of that plant and the rhythm of its species, that is, images of the plants that had gone before and that would follow. You would see this not only on the level of forms but you would see the formless aspect of that life cycle, the energies, the light, the processes that sustain the life of the plant and nourish it in growth, extending from the emergence of that species from a primal source to its ultimate transformation into a different state when that species has fulfilled its planetary purposes. You would see past, present and future all at once.

All created forms have such an image at their heart, and this may be called their identity. In the work of the nature spirits, this image is attuned to and a specific relationship is established to draw out of it what is particularly required to blend with the unfoldment of all the other images that surround it. In this fashion, the ecology of the environment is created. Thus, as a relationship is established between the qualities of soil, rain, wind, sunshine and so forth that signify that it is spring and the appropriate complementary qualities within the seed, germination takes place.

That which communicates with you as Limitless Love and Truth may be described on two levels of existence. In its primary state, it is the image of humanity. As such, it transcends the New Age, encompassing all that humanity has been, back to its source, and all that it will be, on into cosmic dimensions of life beyond this planet. Thus, aspects of this image relate to this earth and aspects relate to other dimensions transcending earth. In its secondary state, this presence is the Deva of the New Age, embodying the specific qualities of timing which determine what needs to be unfolded from the primary image at this time in order to begin a new stage of development.

All who serve in the network of world servers, those who consciously or unconsciously seek to embody this next step and help a new world come into being, are in attunement with this presence. This attunement is through life itself, through the inner qualities of heart and mind. This presence is not oriented to verbal communication, nor can it communicate wholly through any one source, whether it is a person or a group. It is global. It communicates through many ways, but primarily as life and as the energies of loving through which each man and woman and the groups they form externalize the potentials of their seed-identity. It communicates through the actualization of itself through those insights, activities and attitudes which altogether contribute to the next evolutionary step for humanity.

We will now bring this energy forward into the focus of your attention. By personifying it, by verbalizing it and placing it in this particular context, we acknowledge that it becomes limited; however, this is creative focusing that permits this universal presence to become more relevant to your particular identities, becoming an element of consciousness that you and others can relate to through the form of the words. If these words are not taken as final but are seen as signposts, then our work can proceed properly. It is important for people to become aware of this presence and force as a conscious seed within themselves, *as* themselves: their very lives and beings seeking emergence.

Chapter 23

The Image of the New World: Limitless Love and Truth

January 8, 1975

I bless you. I bring you peace, I bring you love, I bring you affirmation of the identity which we share.

I am the Spirit of your deeper selves seeking birth at this time. I am the Spirit of a new world which we can create together. Together we are limitless, for the measures of time and space cannot contain nor delimit what I am within you each and what we are together in co-creative potential. I am that part of each of you and of your world that stands beyond space and time. Hence, my limitlessness is beyond dimension but it seeks entry into dimensionality. I am love, for love is the essence that unites the limitations of your various forms, the various parts that make up the universe, and reveals the limitlessness within, the wholeness that we are. I am truth, which is the life of our identity externalizing itself. For there is only one reality, vaster than all the forms that express it, and that is the I Am That I Am, the identity from which you each emerge in your particularity and which we share and co-express in our oneness.

You are each the wholeness of the universe. You are each a part of it which, blended with other parts in love and truth, in communion and clear identity, makes possible the revelation and emergence of the greater wholeness that encompasses the universe.

As the Spirit of the new, I am not being brought into birth. I am. I am neither born nor do I die. Rather, I am that which directs your attention to that primal quality of beingness out of which the cycles of birth and death themselves emerge and which gives those cycles meaning, direction and purpose. Yet, I am also the promise of a new world which is here now in potential and in spirit; it is about you, within you, upon the etheric, within your thoughts, within your feelings, within your

225

dreams, within your bodies, within your souls. It is obscured by the world which is accepted as reality but which is only a part of reality. I am the Spirit that would free it from that obscurity, saying, "Live My Life, be what I Am, and together we will co-create this world which is *our* life, which is *our* 'I-Am-ness', which is the embodiment and the witness of *our* co-creative identities."

When I spoke with you in our first transmissions in previous years, I spoke that my revelation was complete. It has always been complete, for I was revealed when humanity was born, and I will be revealed when the last man and the last woman reflect the fulfilment of humanity's place in the divine scheme and, having reached that reflection, that fulfilment, transform into something of which you now have no knowledge. Then I will cease to be. Yet, I will become something greater still, a new seed, a new image for which you have no word but which is beyond humanity as you know it while being the son or the creation of humanity.

At that time, I spoke of two worlds, one disintegrating, one building and integrating. I asked for your consciousness to attune to that which is building, for it includes that which is disintegrating within its scope as the seed draws on the compost of plants that have gone before and now return to primal elements. There need be no conflict between these two worlds. This transformation is not a challenge of conflict as much as of perception of higher, vaster states of reality and of embodiment of those states. A person who would move into the new must surrender identification with the old, but he must paradoxically also surrender his identification and attachment with his images of the new or what he thinks to be the new. Such persons must strive to find their identity with what I am, with that which is limitless, beyond time and space: the seed, the source, the image, the identity that is beyond transformation and yet is its cause and its direction.

The route to the New Age is not across the battlefield of conflict, destruction and catastrophe. If the New Age is likened to a different room in a house from the one in which

226

humanity presently dwells, then the route to the New Age is not to pass from the old room to the new but to step out of the house altogether. It is to see the house in wholeness, to see that which is the identity and dream of humanity seeking emergence which encompasses such vast spans of time, of change and cycles, that it cannot be confined to a single age or a single room. It is the whole, and all rooms have their place within it; to understand the place of any room needs understanding of the house itself. Humanity seeks to become attuned to its source identity in full consciousness, to be a lord of its household and not just the dweller within a single room. With that vision, it may then step into or create the room that is new. More appropriately, by understanding and living such a vision, humanity will find itself automatically in that room.

In one sense, I am like a child, for paradoxically, while what I am cannot be born, what I am must be progressively revealed because any moment of time cannot encompass my completeness. It must reflect what is my wholeness, my right relationship to that moment and then give way to the wholeness of the next moment which is thus revealed. This is the process of transformation, of emerging through forms of time and space, of continual rebirth and co-creativity.

Therefore, you may look upon me and what I am within you, as you learn of me and of our relationship, as a child. Those who consciously or unconsciously strive to embody what I am, a network and community of world servers and co-creators, are my parents but all humanity is my womb.

If we use this image, however, then humanity, too, must become like the child. It must be both parent and child, that which is and that which is becoming. It must be Mary and Joseph and the Christ together, for I am revealed through that which is new and through that which has been and is a foundation for revelation. I am a child because the forms that will now express me — and yourselves — are immature and in the earliest stages of development. You are a child in your need to simplify and open yourselves to the wonder and accessibility of the youthful consciousness which does not filter out reality through the preconceptions of the adult. The forms that expressed me in the past, in other cultures and in other times, are the seeds and the compost from which new forms can grow. They are what I am as parent to myself. You are my parents through your wisdom, your experience, your attunement to the rhythms of planetary and human evolution, through your ability to be the stability and the nourishment which protects and nurtures the child.

There cannot be conflict between the parent and the child, between the past and the future, for both are part of the wholeness, the synergy of what I am and of what we could co-create. There must be right relationship between what has been and what is now emerging; it is only through the wisdom within you, the wisdom of your humanity and your divinity, illumined by what I am within you as love and truth, that this right creative relationship can be established.

I have been expressed in many ways by the sons and daughters of humanity throughout your history. Always my emergence comes from a vision of the human potential to reach and to blend with the divine, and from that numinous source — abstract, formless yet compelling — the different races and cultures of humanity have created the forms to give me birth as they have understood that birth . . . to give birth to the highest within themselves.

Many of these forms are no longer adequate or expressive of those potentials. They now crumble and shatter, but the patterns about which these forms once developed, the hope, the image, the promise of divinity, remain true and still seek expression. I am those patterns, the seed of humanity. As the cultures of your world disintegrate, I am there to reveal again the light of this inner destiny and to be the birth of a new culture uniting your planet in wholeness.

I will give you an example of this. Your country of America was begun through an attunement to what I am, an image of the human potential to co-create a society not through hierarchy but through the mutual respect and cooperation of the people. In the idea of democracy, a truth resides that expresses an aspect of humanity's seed-identity. Much that your country has built upon that initial image limits it now and must fall away; you will perceive a new understanding of democracy which your pioneers were not prepared to perceive. Yet, the image they attuned to remains and is strong and true. It is behind and beyond political ideologies and social patterns and it will be revitalized and recommunicated to your world, for that is your country's destiny.

The guiding images of other countries, of other cultures, of other political and economic systems, also come from a bedrock of truth, an attunement to what I am; they have also become encrusted with distortions. As that encrustation is shattered, it will be seen that behind all these images I am, that they are complementary truths expressing a oneness. Humanity will begin to see itself as a single being, a wholeness upon your world, a planetary citizen reaching to cosmic dimensions beyond. With this vision, humanity will free itself from certain bondages to space and time, to the geographical and temporal identities of various cultures; for each people has its land and its history, but now it must be seen that these lands and histories stem from one world and one image seeking externalization through time. From this realization, planetary culture will emerge.

Therefore, I reach out to the sons and daughters of humanity to affirm that they are a unity in love and truth and that a new world can exist for them because it exists in the essence of all they are. Its existence is stronger than the images of the destruction of the old world, for destruction is not an act unto itself but the by-product of co-creating the new. Attention should not be focussed upon destruction, for in me there is no destruction. There is the emergence of the new, and I call to humanity to rise to that vision, to serve each other, to share and to co-create with what I am within each person and within the world, the sinews, the ligaments, the bones and flesh, the blood and nerves and brain of this new world. I call on you to perceive the etheric outlines of this world and to give them flesh and form through love, wisdom, skill in service, and through truth. I ask you to do this with great flexibility, with joy and with freedom, for what you create must in time embody the many dimensions of humanity and express unity in diversity, and it must, in time, be a seed to give way to still newer ages yet to come.

This is the age of man's maturity, to arise and to recognize that he is responsible for the emergence of his identity, for the development of what he is and for the development and blessing of his world. He is responsibile for what he identifies himself as being and for the images he holds which become the gateways through which his life enters into form. Let me be the image, for I am the image of your identity. Co-create with what I am as love and truth and wholeness. Carry me into expression and affirm yourselves as one with the identity of this new world — not the identity of its forms, for these have yet to be created, but with the identity of its essence, its spirit, and its power, from which those forms will come and are coming. The identity of this world is one in which humanity confronts itself as a divine being and takes on with wisdom and with skill, in wholeness and in love the truth of its identity as a co-creator with God.

Humanity has looked for the images of God. Now it will see that the image of itself and the image of God must blend synergetically, becoming a new image encompassing both. They are not the same image, for there are aspects of divinity which humanity does not embody; it is not the wholeness of God, but God's wholeness is in it. Humanity must find its divinity that is the revelation of that wholeness in complementarity with the divinity of its world and universe, and know its oneness with God. Let mankind know its divine essence and be aware of the multi-dimensionality of its life, aware of its spirit and aware of its forms.

I am that essence, that divinity within yourselves. Identify with me and with the wholeness of yourselves, of your species, of your world. Proclaim that you are the seeds and cells, the life and rhythm, the entry and the womb, the co-creators of a new world.

What this new world shall be like will be discovered and enunciated by many men and women throughout the world, whose voices will grow to become one voice as they recognize their oneness. I am within them all. I am within you each. I am neither of the old world nor of the new; I am of both. I am of all worlds. There is no separation from what I am. As I have said before, I do not preach the kingdom of the lost nor of the saved. Rather I proclaim the kingdom that is within, the kingdom of the image of humanity, which encompasses the worlds of lost and saved and strives to make them one, that men may move from conflict into peace and from limitation into freedom.

Live my Life. Be what I Am. Let us co-create together the world that comes from our beingness.

Chapter 24:

The Image and the Seed —
Growing into the New

The Jewish, Christian and Moslem religions, which form the traditions and set the tone of consciousness and culture for most of the industrialized world and many of the developing countries, are religions of the Book. They are based on sacred writings, the Word of God as inscribed in the Bible and the Koran, and the emphasis is on hearing that Word, recording it, understanding it and obeying it. These religions and their representatives are like the messengers of God, whose message acts as a bridge between humanity and the Divine. Where there is a bridge, though, there is also a chasm. The implication is one of separation.

When this message/messenger orientation is carried to an extreme, the word becomes all-important, and the spirit or living presence may be lost in the form of the syntax and vocabulary. Revelation may be anticipated as the receiving of new words rather than as the arising of a new spirit and consciousness. Such an orientation reflects the general tendency within humanity to prefer and to feel more secure with that which is well-defined, concrete, limited and possessing of definite form rather than with that which seems abstract, open-ended, limitless and formless or with mutable form. If a New Age is being born, we would like to know its shape, its characteristics, the strategies of its birth and development . . . in short, the blueprint of its creation spelled out in clear and precise words. We wish a message that will tell us what to do, how to do it, when and where.

Such an approach and expectation is neither wrong nor incapable of fulfilment. Certainly there are patterns, plans, trends, processes, details and techniques which can be discerned and verbally described; the universe is information in action, generating new information, and we live in a rich ocean of messages: creation is communication. On the other hand, there is a reverse side to the message/messenger orientation to the co-creative relationship between God and humanity, the Whole and the Part. This is the being/embodiment relationship, as exemplified primarily in the Eastern religions and philosophies and certain aspects of the esoteric and mystical traditions. This relationship simply affirms that all life is one, that I am one with God and can embody Divinity, and that the messages of God are messages from a vaster aspect of the one Being reminding me of our union and calling me to oneness. God and I do not just communicate; we commune and are one. There is no separation except failure to recognize that there is no separation. Revelation is the progressive unfoldment of God's presence within me and of my capacity to embody it as my true identity.

The truth of our relationship with the whole lies in the synthesis of these two approaches. We must learn of our identity and learn to know and be the oneness of creation; we must also learn to listen, to communicate and to "speak the Word," or project our life and essence into precise and structured forms when this is necessary.

The understanding of this is essential for evaluation of the transmissions of Limitless Love and Truth. This is a book, and the transmissions are in words; they are a message. Influenced by a message/messenger orientation to spiritual truth, we could be dominated by the words, either accepting them too fully as truth themselves or finding fault and incompleteness in them and rejecting them as truth. Yet, the transmissions themselves say, *I am beyond words;* and, most importantly, *Live my life, Be what I AM!*

There is another reason for this understanding, and that lies in the nature of the process by which I co-expressed these communications. In a way, this book places me in the position of being a prophet. If so, I am not saying, "Here is the Word of the Divine!"; rather, I am saying, "Here is an image of our Divinity!" This is literally my experience of this process. As I described in Chapter 3, this attunement is a communion and

233

co-mingling of identities, a synergy that creates a new identity that is more than what I am as David Spangler, more than what the presence is that is that is communing with me. For me, this is the experience of a living image, an embodied idea, a presence of love and truth. It influences and sometimes guides the concepts, words, phrasing and so forth which become the verbal representation of that image, but I am not experiencing words. I must help choose words to describe as best I can a living dynamic reality. Ninety percent of the time, the true purpose and communication arising out of my contacts with higher levels is the transmission of an energy, a living force, an image; words are only vehicles to facilitate this transmission, like microwaves that permit the broadcasting of television pictures. As vehicles, they must be appropriate to their function but must always be considered in relationship to the greater wholeness of meaning and dynamic life which they represent as specific forms in time and place.

This book, therefore, is less of a message and more of a sharing of the experience of an image. This is the image of our Divinity, of our co-creative relationship with each other and with other aspects of the whole of life, and of the new world that can emerge out of a proper embodiment of that relationship. This new world, this new age, exists. It is whether as a seed, an image or as an etheric reality. Our task at first is not to build it but to perceive it; not to plan for it but to understand it; not to create it but to be it. Out of perception, out of understanding, out of being, it will emerge. The seed will grow; the image will come into focus.

If this seems like wishful thinking or an impractical procedure, it is not. It is the organic manner in which all the world has come into being as a responsible and responsive unfoldment of inner identity. In our Western culture, we are taught the value and necessity of action, a valuable teaching, to be sure. On the other hand, the best action is sometimes not outward or physical; it is inward and reflective. It is the apparent non-action of providing clear, quiet space for something to emerge. When there is a need for new insights, new images to guide us in our creativity, this is the most valuable action of all.

All the words, all the philosophies cannot mask the fact that we do and create according to what we are or think we are. Revelation provides one glimpse of a new image of our beingness, out of which new creativity can grow. The new world is a seed within us; our responsibility is to be proper husbanders of that seed. The new age is a will-to-act within us; our responsibility is to act with wisdom and appropriateness to that which we would co-create. This is our task as individuals and our task together. Messiahs may appear, but they cannot do this work for us. The image is in us all. We must learn to give it birth, for it is our identity, after all.

There are many who are doing this. Since leaving Findhorn, Myrtle and I and others with whom we work have had increasing contact with a growing network of groups and individuals working in every field of society and knowledge — politics, business, religion, art, education, the esoteric traditions, parapsychology, psychology — to create spaces for the emergence of this image. The new world is appearing in our midst, even as Limitless Love and Truth proclaimed.

Words come to an end (and often, thankfully so!), but revelation goes on, for it is our evolving Identity in action. This last part of this book indicates that, in a specific sense, contact with Limitless Love and Truth did not stop with the Findhorn experience, nor is it limited to that center. It is limitless and on-going, and we are all part of it. It is a living promise, and we are the embodiments of that promise: we are the Word of Revelation made flesh. We are the message. Now and always.

In the seed and image of Limitless Love and Truth: *You are my Beloveds and I am with you always. At the end of an age, at the beginning of an age, and beyond — beyond time, beyond form — we are One. So it is, so it has been, so it shall always be. Live my life. Be what I AM. Let us co-create together the world that comes from our beingness.*

Let Revelation continue!

A Prayer

Our Beloved, placed about our shoulders is the mantle of Love and upon us the crown of Truth and within us the Life which bears these things in perfection, in balance and in oneness with all that You are. We rejoice in this oneness with all the kingdoms of life and the expressions of Your Being and we seek to unite with them to form together a new heaven and a new earth. So be it.

I finished the material for this new edition of *Revelation* in August of 1975 and turned it over to Ira Friedlander of Rainbow Bridge with a sense of satisfied completion. Now, I could turn my attention wholly to the on-going work of writing my second book, *Emergence*, and to the development of Lorian, the non-profit, religious educational corporation Myrtle and I and a small group of friends from our Findhorn experience were attempting to co-create. However, as the autumn came and slid almost imperceptibly into the California winter, that satisfaction began to give way to a feeling of incompleteness. In some way, I had not really finished this book.

Part of this feeling came from the fact that the processes behind *Revelation* are very dynamic, as I have tried to suggest in the last chapters. They do not end; rather, they manifest a continuing unfoldment reflected in the growth of consciousness within people. From the time I completed the last page of Chapter 24 and bundled the manuscript together to give to Ira, more insight, more information, more experience of the processes involved in giving birth to a "New Age" has continued to come. I would not have it otherwise for any of us, for that is what life is all about. However, it wasn't from this that the feeling of incompleteness stemmed. *Emergence* is providing an adequate vehicle to contain and express these on-going insights, in some ways better than this book could have done. I know, too, that there will be other books, other ways of expressing the continuation of growth and exploration into the transformations of our times. I feel no compulsion to pack everything I know or am learning into this present book which you have finished reading.

On the other hand, both the work on *Emergence* and on Lorian have compelled me to look more deeply (or perhaps in a different and more objective way) into this phenomenon we are calling the New Age. The purpose of this has not been to get more data or information or to make predictions or blueprints about the future. Rather, it has been to gain a sense of perspective about the *context* in which this phenomenon is occuring. It is easy (and far too common, I have found) to think of the New Age as an event and in terms of change. However, it is much more than an event in space and time, and it is rooted in a more fundamental reality than just change from one state or consciousness to another. We may miss this deeper reality, however, and consequently blunt the force of transformation because our thoughts and feelings — our whole conceptual framework — is so oriented to seeing change, growth and evolution as processes of sequential cause and effect relationships. The important questions of our time may not be, "What are we changing into?" or "What are the processes of transformation?" Instead, the important questions may be "What does it mean to change?" or "Can I recognize a real process of transformation when I see it; what is change?" Of course, when examined, we see that these questions arise from a more fundamental one, which is, "Who or what am I and what is my role in a dynamic universe?" Before we can know the direction and mechanics of change, we need to know what it is that is changing. Therefore, the idea of a New Age has meaning not so much in terms of what has been or what may be coming but rather in terms of what is. That is the context of which I am speaking: the nature of ourselves, the nature of reality; for we can only understand and participate co-creatively with the processes of transformation to the extent that we are clearly and intelligently perceiving that nature.

It has been my observation that the whole realm of activity, debate and exploration about the New Age idea generally occupies too shallow a level; it does not penetrate deeply enough into the heart of the matter. We become concerned with matters which, while undoubtedly important, nevertheless fail to carry a significantly transformative energy; they fail to be sufficiently rooted in and alive to that context of beingness that embraces and transcends this particular

238

moment in the historical relationship between the manifest and the unmanifest. We try to understand the New Age in terms of new forms, new teachings, new revelation, new information, new consciousness (by which we often mean only new *images* or *ideas* about what consciousness is or should be); we think about the New Age, we try to feel into it emotively, but we often fail to experience it because we fail to experience ourselves. Not knowing who we are and our function in a living, dynamic universe, we fall short of knowing what the New Age is or how to really bring it into being.

This is not a new struggle. There have been many such crisis points in human history before. We are continuing an ancient dialogue between ourselves and life, the purpose of which is an intimate knowing we have yet to achieve. In the Old Testament, "knowing" is used as a euphimism for sexual intercourse, and perhaps this is an appropriate use of this word, for to truly know something or someone is to achieve a deep and intimate unity with that thing or person; it is to share an identity, as symbolized by sexual union but as rarely achieved because of our narrow concretization of the idea of sex and our limiting it to a physical act or event. To know who we are, both in ourselves and in the universe, is to participate deeply in a wholeness, a unity, a shared or unified identity. This is the knowing we seek, and it is a knowing often blunted by a superficial attraction on intellectual and emotional levels to ideas and feelings, especially when they are part of the glamorous context of a New Age.

I can only suggest the direction of these thoughts at this time, for to go more deeply into them would be to write another book, which, in fact, is what *Emergence* is all about. However, because I have been reflecting in my own mind on the transmissions from Limitless Love and Truth within the light of these thoughts over the past few months, I have felt it important to share that reflection with you. This is especially so when I think of the potential of these transmissions to be taken on too shallow a level as well. As I have said elsewhere, there is a glamor about communication with other levels that can completely obscure the transformative purpose of such communication. To believe or to disbelieve, or to evolve a cosmology, a theosophy or theology about such communications is to engage in the creation and processing of mental and emotional contents but does not necessarily lead to the kind of *knowing* which creates new life (or which creates life, period.)

In pursuing these reflections, three ideas stand out that I feel should be shared as an afterword to this book and as a foreword to the processes that lie beyond this book.

First, a word about Findhorn and the function of tradition. There is a tendency to see tradition as a synonym for that which is crystallized, stagnating, enclosed, old, unable to move into the new, and so forth. Certainly, when we view tradition through the veil of the fabrics we have woven to clothe it throughout history, such connotations may be justified. Traditional institutions — the vehicles through which tradition is transmitted through time — may well become outmoded and obstructionist. Tradition itself, however, is a timeless vitality, the presence of truth, where truth is defined as the process of *knowing*, the instrumentality for union and wholeness of identity, both within "myself" and between "me" and the "universe." All civilization and culture has that tradition at its heart and begins to fail only when it loses the clear connection with that heart. The cholesterol of undigested ideas and emotions begin to clog the living arteries, and the vitality of the heart is denied to the body. Then we see tradition as that which is clogging ("There are circulatory problems.") rather than as that which is being clogged.

In an attempt to rectify this, we seek out pathways back to the heart, back to the center. We may do this by delving into the mysteries of the past, the sacred traditions of ancient cultures, or by going to other lands and other civilizations to find connections we cannot find in our own. Since the Tradition itself is timeless and universal, it is quite possible that such a quest will, by changing our perspective and forcing

240

us to look, think and feel more deeply, enable us to make that contact. It is also likely that we will simply add more undigested content to ourselves, tapping only the cholesterol levels of other civilizations and thus increasing the state of clogging while maintaining an illusion of contact with something deeper. "New" and "different" are not necessarily deeper and more real.

In this context, it may make sense to say that Tradition is never traditional. What we call tradition is, in its highest sense, a scaffolding of physical, psychological and spiritual techniques and insights designed to lift us into the presence of the universal Tradition or truth. That truth is a radical element in our lives; it comes from beyond time and space, from beyond dimension. It draws us into a place where we confront the wholeness, the Light, and unless we are prepared for that confrontation, we can easily be destroyed by our inability to assimilate or sustain such wholeness or identity. Thus, Tradition extends itself into traditions that sequentially prepare us for that meeting with the Presence, that *knowing* with ourselves, that mating with the infinite. What many are sensing in our time and referring to as the birth of a New Age or the descent of new energies and revelations is the unfoldment of more appropriate pathways of preparation for, and confrontation with, *knowing*. Is it possible, in other terms, to relate to God and Divinity (two synonyms for this Tradition, Presence or truth) in a new and perhaps more direct or relevant way? In answering that question we must also answer anew who we are and what is this reality we call God.

Findhorn confronts us directly with this question. There are many ways one can approach and relate to this community: through the garden, through its educational aspect, through its esoteric aspects (contact with elementals, with Masters, etc.), through its creative opportunities or through the community life itself. However, all these are subsidiary to Findhorn's one, deep reality: it is a God-centered, God-directed community.

Long before Limitless Love and Truth appeared on the

241

scene as a communicator through the beingness of David Spangler, long before Findhorn itself appeared, Eileen and Peter and Dorothy had been experiencing contact with their Divinity. For Eileen, it was in the form of a voice within her that gave counsel and direction. It is significant to me that Findhorn grew out of that contact, rather than out of contact with some personified identity, such as a Master or an angel. To be God-directed, in the simple, yet profound way that the Caddy's experienced, cut through metaphysical and occult complexities and presented the onlooker with the question of a person's relationship to the Center, to the Presence, rather than to a peripheral manifestation of that Center. In this sense, Findhorn was built on a direct apprehension of Tradition rather than on reliance on one of the many traditions that seek to express the Presence.

Of course, the question arose many times among visitors as to whether Eileen really was in contact with God or how clear and pure that contact might be. To me, though, this was not the essential matter, which was, rather, that through Eileen and Peter and Dorothy, one was again confronted with the possibility of such a contact. To judge their contact as a matter of belief or disbelief is to evade the essential issue. Only by dealing with the possibility of an inner Divinity and by exploring the nature of contact with it within oneself could a person approach a position of discernment. Having allowed that possibility to live within oneself, then the question of how to approach that Center could be legitimately considered. Findhorn is still exploring the emergence of new processes of contact with Divinity within a community setting.

How they are doing that is not my theme here. I simply want to make this point, which I feel is important in evaluating the Findhorn experiment: the function of all traditions is to bring us safely and wholly into the presence of the Tradition, or, if you prefer, into the *knowing* of that God-Presence which embraces ourselves and the universe and is dynamic reality. This is often overlooked as we seek paths of transformation for ouselves and our world; we become caught on the level of the ideas, emotions and techniques of the sacred traditions (or modern ones, such as psychotherapy in its many forms). We are relating to lesser manifestations: psychic powers, new ideas, an integrated personality, growth, and so forth, all the time circling but not penetrating the core of it all. We follow the direction of our passive mind that seeks out what attracts it and is a prisoner of the search. We are like a sperm that would prefer to keep swimming than to penetrate the egg, blending itself in the co-creation of a new identity. At Findhorn, such evasion of the center is possible, but it is not so easy, for the "tradition" of Findhorn is to be in the Presence of God, to embody that Presence, to confront the ultimate purpose of the traditions and to keep that purpose fully in mind even while (and especially while) working out the details of the process. The community acts as a mirror in which each person must learn to see himself and herself as he and she is in relationship to life, not necessarily in the form of confrontation but to facilitate *knowing*. This, too, meets the needs of the Tradition when properly exercised, for to know the Presence is to know oneself, and vice versa.

Second, it is fruitless to compare the Limitless Love and Truth transmissions with, say, Eileen's guidance or Dorothy's messages from the Devas. They are all manifesting this same impulse. The value of Eileen's contact is not her guidance; that has value only on a pragmatic level, important to be sure but limited to specific objectives in time and space. The value lies in the archetype of the contact itself, as a mirror of the meaning of Tradition and a suggestion of how to realign oneself with the right use of the sacred traditions. This is also true of my transmissions. Limitless Love and Truth is also a signpost to the Center, which is love and truth. We are asked to be that Presence, to live its life. How? We each must discover that, but the point is less how to do it and more what it is we are trying to do. If we don't know how to live that life, is it not because we don't really understand what love and truth are as living, universal qualities? Therefore, our first step must be to question and to look deeply to see what love is and what truth is in a universal context. Is love only a quality of relationship? Is truth only a measure of the rightness of the content of our beings and its lack of distortion or falsity? Or are both these terms really referring to something very substantial and essential to the framework of reality? Might truth not be the process that unites us with the universe, that enables us to *know*, and thus enables us to BE? Might love not be the quality that permits us to sustain that beingness and not be shattered into fragments, the wholeness that allows us to enter the presence of truth? Are love and truth only ways in which I can relate to my world or are they aspects of my very self? These are the questions I must use as guidelines as I seek to make my life and my world a yoga for my approach to Tradition. Otherwise, Limitless Love and Truth becomes only something else to believe in or not, as my personality determines on the basis of what is attractive and what is not.

Finally, the third reflection I have had these past months concerns the process of giving birth to a New Age and arises out of our attempts as a group to define the role and identity of Lorian. Our world is condemned for being too dense, too materialistic, too concrete, and we may yearn for a more refined, spiritual reality (whatever that means to us). However, the process of concretization, of manifestation and materialization is part of the whole. It is an essential part of creation. Our challenge is to know how to materialize in timing. We can concretize something too quickly, resulting in either stillbirth or a malformed product, or we can hesitate too long, or we can try to concretize everything, forgetting that we live in a universe of levels.

Many concerned groups that I have met are trying to bring the New Age into manifestation, to draw up blueprints for Aquarius, to chart the course of our future, but are doing so primarily out of a desire to take action. A comparatively fewer number are actually thinking deeply about transformation and its implications, not just in terms of change and movement through time and history, but in terms of being and the meaning of life. They are seeking to go beyond activity to a deeper level of understanding. That is the greater context of which I spoke earlier. Without adding the illumination of this context to our action, there is a danger of concretizing that which should not be or of concretizing too quickly, before we have had a chance to really discriminate and see what the new patterns may be that are seeking birth. We materialize out of the level of our fears, needs, glamors and instincts rather than out of a deep attunement to the essential seed-identity within ourselves and our planet, as the most recent transmission alluded to.

When we returned from Findhorn, a group of us formed Lorian with the idea of materializing some kind of organization. As this course became blocked, it gradually became clear that an important part of the process of transformation and emergence is what could be called a pause or space between the manifest and the unmanifest, between idea and form. It is in that space that it is possible to touch a common source of being, our timelessness, and gain a sense of what is happening or seeking to happen. It is that moment's reflection in our own experience which makes the difference between reaction and directed action: the "counting to ten" that separates us from just doing or engaging in activity without the added and necessary dimension of creative awareness.

Our Western culture, particularly in America, puts a value on action; we even see it as the opposite of contemplation, which is a ridiculous perception for anyone who understands the synthesis of the two that allows for truly transformative activity. This tendency can make us turn the New Age into just another variation of the myth of endless and inevitable progress, translated into a somewhat esoteric framework. What we need is to cultivate that process of reflection that can illuminate action.

Lorian has ceased to be a group or a movement toward a community (although groups and communities could arise out of its process of reflection). Instead, it has become an educational experiment in embodying that space between idea and incarnation. Through its journal and other media, it seeks to reflect on the larger context of the New Age, just as I have been reflecting on it with you in this "after-forward." Through working through a group process (and past many desires and pressures to "get something going" or manifesting on the outer), we have gained an insight into the importance of this reflection in implementing the birth of a New Age.

To reflect well means that the mirror is polished, and that can require discipline and a sense of what one is doing; it is not the same as simply allowing for a stream of consciousness. In some ways to enter that space is the hardest activity of all until one is used to it. It has always been the function of traditions to help us know how to enter that space and how to recognize it from its imitators. At the heart of this function have been the people who can embody it: people are our mirrors; the Tradition is embodied in us. That is why community is an important tool in this birthing process, for it can provide a mechanism for reflection and discipline.

Not everyone can go to an intentional community, but we are all part of a communicating universe. We must communicate with each other, with work programs, with family members, with life, with ourselves. I believe the Aquarian Age is one in which the skills of true communication will be seen as a primal building block of creation. Thus, around us always are opportunities to see ourselves and to help others to see as well, chances to polish our mirrors so that they reflect truly. We have chances to listen, chances to talk, chances to enter into the discipline of communication which seems so little understood and which is the essence of our environment. We live in — are part of — an ocean of communicating energies which strive to create the deepest communication of all, which is communion, knowing and identity. It is this awareness of communication and its discipline or process that is the birth channel for the New Age. We must learn to communicate together in order to bring it into form, but also we must learn who we are as

246

communicants, and we must pause to listen to that "still, small voice" through which our life, our world, our New Age seeks to communicate what it is and can become.

David Spangler
Belmont, California, USA
January, 1976

Suggested Reading List
(and other points of further contact)

Following are some books and some other points of contact with the image and growth of a new age with which I am familiar and can recommend. The list is kept short, but it could form a book in itself. Hopefully, these will be points of entry for you into that greater world of emergence, after which you will undoubtedly find your own best way.

BOOKS ON NEW VISIONS OF OURSELVES, OF SOCIETY AND OF REALITY

BAILEY, Alice A. *Initiation Human and Solar.* Lucis Publishing Company. (this is the first of several books on esoteric reality produced by Alice Bailey in co-operation with a Tibetan initiate. She founded the Lucis Trust, which provides correspondence courses and other services to interested seekers.)

CAPRA, Fritjof. *The Tao of Physics.* Shambhala. (A book on the parallels between modern physics and Eastern mysticism by a theoretical physicist.)

CERMINARA, Gina. *Insights for the Age of Aquarius.* Prentice-Hall. (An investigation into religion and the development of new spiritual attitudes using the science of General Semantics.)

KOESTLER, Arthur. *The Roots of Coincidence.* Vintage paperback. (A look at the relationship between quantum physics and parapsychological phenomena: an excellent description of what might be called the "mysticism of physics".)

KUHN, Thomas. *The Structure of Scientific Revolutions.* University of Chicago Press. (A look at the phenomenon of transformation of consciousness, using the history of science as the theme.)

LeSHAN, Lawrence. *The Medium, they Mystic, and the Physicist.* Viking. (Describes the convergence of the reality views of mysticism, psychic attunement and physics.)

LASZLO, Ervin. *The Systems View of the World.* Braziller. (Describes the developing science of General Systems Theory, which is one of the embodiments of a new, dynamic, holistic view of reality.)

MARUYAMA, Magoroh & HARKINS, Arthur. *Cultures Beyond the Earth: The Role of Anthropology in Outer Space.* Vintage paperback. (An unusual book of anthropological essays intended to stretch one's perspectives and mirror our own culture in new ways.)

ORNSTEIN, Robert E. *The Psychology of Consciousness.* Freeman. (A look at new research into the nature of our consciousness, written in an engaging and intuition-provoking style, also drawing on mystical and esoteric sources such as Sufism.)

PEARCE, Joseph. *The Crack in the Cosmic Egg* and *Exploring the Crack in the Cosmic Egg*. Julian Press. (These books directly explore the nature of reality and the role of consciousness in creating it.)

PEARSON, E. Norman. *Space, Time and Self*. Quest Publishers. (An excellent survey of the basic esoteric philosophy of Theosophy.)

ROSZAK, Theodore. *Where the Wasteland Ends*. Anchor paperback. (An examination of transformation and the beginning of a new culture.)

SINCLAIR, John R. *The Other Universe*. Rider. (A look at the esoteric wisdoms in relation to societal transformation, among other things. A good look at the esoteric movement and tradition.)

SMITH, E. Lester. (Ed.) *Intelligence Came First*. Quest Publishers. (Written by a group of British scientists giving evidence that the essence of intelligence existed before and brought about the development of the brain; a new look at evolution.)

STEIGER, Brad & WHITE, John (Eds.) *Other Worlds, Other Universes*. Doubleday. (A book on various reality views, including a chapter of my own on "Planetary Transformation and the Myth of the Extra-Terrestrial.")

THOMAS, Lewis. *The Lives of a Cell — Notes of a Biology Watcher*. Viking. (This is one of my favorite books simply for expanding our perspective of the life we live, the complex community of lives which we are, the universe in which we grow, and so forth; it is excellently written.)

TOBEN, Bob. *Space-Time and Beyond*. Dutton paperback. (A delightful illustrated introduction to the new reality views being opened up by the convergence of advanced scientific thinking and ancient esoteric insights. It also contains an excellent reading list for further exploration.)

WHITE, John. (Ed.) *Frontiers of Consciousness*. Julian Press. (A collection of articles exploring the theme of the title, introducing the frontiers of the new world rapidly emerging about us.)

WILSON, Colin. *New Pathways in Psychology*. Taplinger. paperback. (A fine introduction and survey to the new fields of humanistic and transpersonal psychologies which explore the potentials and frontiers of human nature and the soul.)

BOOKS ON THE NEW AGE, PLANETARY TRANSFORMATION, THE NEW CULTURE AND THE FUTURE

BAILEY, Alice A. *The Reappearance of the Christ*. Lucis. (A challenging look at the nature of the Christ and His work in co-creating a new civilization.)

BATESON, Mary Catherine. *Our Own Metaphor.* Knopf. (A personal account of a conference on the role of human purpose, consciousness and will on human adaptation and evolution towards a better future.)

DESAN, Wilfrid. *The Planetary Man.* Macmillan. (A philosophical investigation of the planetary or universal dimensions of individual man, a "search for a re-definition of man within the changing climate of our world." This book pays off for those willing to invest the time to read it deeply.)

ELLWOOD, Robert S. *Religious and Spiritual Groups in Modern America.* Prentice-Hall. (An excellent survey of a number of "New Age" and esoteric/occult groups in America, giving a flavor of an aspect of the emergence of a new age.)

FERKISS, Victor. *The Future of Technological Civilization.* Braziller. (A look at the new philosophy of man/technology/ecology relationships necessary to permit a new civilization to emerge.)

FINDHORN FOUNDATION. *The Findhorn Garden.* Harper & Row. (An excellent book about the development of the Findhorn garden and community and the relationship between humanity and nature, written by members of the community.)

HAWKEN, Paul. *The Magic of Findhorn.* Harper & Row. (A well-written personal account of the author's visit to Findhorn, his impressions of the community, its history and development and the stories of the Caddys, Dorothy Maclean, ROC, and others of the founders and builders of Findhorn.)

JANTSCH, Erich. *Design for Evolution.* Braziller. (A somewhat technical book on the theme of co-creativity, the evolution of consciousness, drawing on silence, General Systems Theory, mythology, esoterica, mysticism, Zen, psychology, etc.)

LEONARD, George. *The Transformation.* Delacorte. (Subtitled, "A guide to the inevitable changes in Humankind." A very readable introduction to the changes of our time in consciousness and in society.)

MESAROVIC, Mihajlo and PESTEL, Eduard. *Mankind at the Turning Point.* Dutton/Reader's Digest Press. (The second report to the Club of Rome, an analysis of the forces leading us to the need for radical transformation and the development of new visions for society.)

NEEDLEMAN, Jacob. *The New Religions.* Pocket Books Paperback.

.... *A Sense of the Cosmos: The Encounter of Modern Science and Ancient Truth.* Doubleday. (I consider both of these books basic reading for anyone seeking to understand the phenomena and processes of transformation and the eternal relationship of the individual to the universe. The second book in particular asks and discusses the kind of questions that must be dealt with if we are truly to have a "New Age and a New Humanity.")

POLAK, Fred. *Images of the Future.* Elsevier. Translated by Elise Boulding. (An excellent analysis of the role of images of the future in the life and creativity of cultures, with an historical survey of such images, which served as the "New Age images" for past cultures. It throws light on the importance and the antecedents of the New Age image in our time.)

ROSZAK, Theodore. *Unfinished Animal: The Aquarian Frontier and the Evolution of Consciousness.* Harper & Row. (Another book which I consider basic reading for anyone wanting to understand and evaluate our time of transition. It is a comprehensive survey of the new spiritual movement and what may lie behind it.)

RUDHYAR, Dane. *The Planetarization of Consciousness — From the Individual to the Whole.* Harper Colophon Books (paperback)
　　We Can Begin Again Together. Omen Communications, Inc.
　　Occult Preparations for a New Age. Quest Publishers. (These three books by a forward thinking philosopher are basic to exploring the new attitudes and consciousness emerging as the New Age. Strategies of transformation are also discussed. — An excellent presentation of a holistic world view.)

SALK, Jonas. *The Survival of the Wisest.* Harper & Row. (Another well-written book on transformation and revisioning our future, in this case with supportive images drawn from the biological sciences.)

SCHUMACHER, E.F. *Small is Beautiful — Economics as if People Mattered.* Harper Torchbooks (paperback). (A collection of essays by a world-famous economist, exploring the economics of a new age.)

THOMPSON, William Irwin. *At the Edge of History* and *Passages About Earth: An Exploration of the New Planetary Culture.* Harper & Row. (These are two excellent books by a mystically-inclined cultural historian, examining the forces of consciousness and history that are bringing one cycle of human experience to an end and inaugurating a new one.)

WAGAR, W. Warren. *Building the City of Man: Outlines of a World Civilization.* Grossman. (A vision of what a possible future planetary civilization might be like; this book is politically, socially and inspirationally oriented, outlining definite strategies for bringing such a civilization into being. You may not share Wagar's specific vision but the book is consciousness-expanding and relates to the need for definite social action to match our ideals.)

252

BOOKS ON PERSONAL TRANSFORMATION

There are many routes to personal transformation, represented by religion, philosophy, psychology, various spiritual disciplines and gurus, meditative techniques, and so forth. I believe we must each find that way which relates us to our seed-Identity, our inner divinity, and helps that to unfold. The following books, like the preceding ones, are not meant as specific recommendations of a particular path but only as starting points. I do not agree with nor practice everything in all these books, but they can be useful catalysts upon our way.

ASSAGIOLI, Roberto. *The Act of Will.* Viking. (A sequel to his book on Psychosynthesis, it describes the often misunderstood nature and function of human will in personal synthesis and transformation.)

CRAIG, James H. and Marge. *SYNERGIC POWER: Beyond Domination and Permissiveness.* Proactive Press. (The only book I've seen applying the principles of synergy to human interaction — politics — and transformation of relationships.)

KARLFRIED, Graf von Durckheim. *Daily Life as Spiritual Exercise: The Way of Transformation.* Harper & Row paperback. (This book addresses itself to making the affairs of daily life a yoga, a means of attunement and transformation.)

DONNELLY, Morwenna. *Founding the Life Divine.* Rider. (This is a very fine introduction to the integral yoga of Sri Aurobindo, a pioneer of the New Age vision. The planetary city of Auroville, near Pondicherry, India, is an outgrowth of his work.)

GOLAS, Thaddeus. *The Lazy Man's Guide to Enlightenment.* Seed Center Publishers, Palo Alto, CA. (This book is fun to read, short and filled with seed thoughts for transformation.)

LeSHAN, Lawrence, *HOW TO MEDITATE: A Guide to Self-Discovery.* Little, Brown. (A very good, sane and simple introduction to the vast field of meditation.)

NARANJO, Claudio. *The One Quest.* Ballantine paperback. (A broad introduction to the field of personal transformation; a good guide-book to the subject.)

and ORNSTEIN, Robert E. *On the Psychology of Meditation.* Viking. (Another fine introduction to the history and practice of meditation.)

PROGOFF, Ira. *At a Journal Workshop.* Dialogue House Library, New York. (An introduction generally to the idea of keeping a journal and writing as an aid to transformation and specifically to the technique of the Intensive Journal as developed by the author, a depth psychologist. He has other books in the field of new consciousness and emergence which you may wish to explore.)

STRONG, Mary. *Letters of the Scattered Brotherhood.* Harper & Row. (A collection of anonymous letters written about the spiritual path and its integration with daily life. Filled with wisdom, this is one of my favorite books which I recommend to everybody.)

FURTHER POINT OF CONTACT

LORIAN is a spiritually-oriented educational association whose aim is to serve the emergence of a new planetary culture.

The Association is researching and evolving educational programs, creative arts presentations, and other services for institutions, specialized groups, and the general public.

Further information on Lorian may be obtained by writing to LORIAN, P.O. Box 1095, ELGIN, ILLINOIS 60120.